Storytelling With Shapes & Numbers

By Valerie Marsh

Illustrated by Patrick K. Luzadder

Alleyside Press

Fort Atkinson, Wisconsin

Published by Alleyside Press,
an imprint of Highsmith Press LLC
Highsmith Press
W5527 Highway 106
P.O. Box 800
Fort Atkinson, Wisconsin 53538-0800
1-800-558-2110

© Valerie Marsh, 1999
Cover design: Frank Neu

The paper used in this publication meets the minimum requirements of
American National Standard for Information Science — Permanence of Paper
for Printed Library Material. ANSI/NISO Z39.48-1992.

Library of Congress Cataloging in Publication
  Marsh, Valerie.
    Storytelling with shapes & numbers / by Valerie Marsh ;
  illustrated by Patrick K. Luzadder.
      p.   cm.
    ISBN 1-57950-024-2 (alk. paper)
    1. Storytelling. 2. Paper work. 3. Shapes. 4. Numerals.
  I. Title. II. Title: Storytelling with shapes and numbers.
  LB1042.M2874 1999
  372.67´7--dc21   99-14237
                                                      CIP

Contents

To creative souls everywhere who know
storytelling and storylistening is an
intriguing way to learn

&

To all children who are learning their
numbers and shapes

Introduction

Why storytelling?

Storytelling is fun! Fun for the listeners and the teller! And one of the best ways to tell a great story is to be a storyteacher! As a storyteacher, you are telling stories for many reasons —enjoyment, appreciation of good literature and development of listening skills. But most importantly, you are demonstrating to children how they themselves can tell stories. This takes the pressure off of you to be a great performer. Instead, you are just doing what you probably do everyday, and that is work with children. When you think of it in this context, storytelling becomes easy. You are a storyteacher. Storyteaching has one main goal—to empower children to enjoy and to tell stories themselves.

Just by listening to your story, children develop higher level thinking skills, including critical thinking, short- and long-term memory, analysis, synthesis, and sequencing. Children also learn to distinguish between reality and fantasy. They gain general knowledge, a better understanding of other cultures, compassion, and self-confidence. Storylistening gives children a chance to develop their creative imagination! Finally, while listening to a story, the listeners and the teller can escape from the real world for a few moments, coming back to it with renewed vigor and increased confidence.

Always be sure to repeat favorite stories. Sometimes in repeating a story, it will become a favorite, but each story deserves to be told at least twice. Of course, the best indicator of which stories to tell comes from your audience, and a child's requests for a particular story should be honored whenever possible.

When should you tell these stories?

- To introduce or conclude a unit of study on a particular number or shape.

- Rewards: Children need to learn that rewards can take forms other than material things such as food and stickers. Rewards can also be active entertainment rather than passive (such as a movie).

- Quiet times after recess or lunch.

- Waiting times between classes or during lunch periods.

- Holiday parties: Choose a story to entertain children at the party.

- Unexpected delays such as waiting for a late speaker during a school convocation.

- Entertainment at a school fair or carnival.

- After-school art and crafts programs.

- After-school child care programs.
- Curriculum integration of art, listening skills, sequencing skills, writing skills and history.

Guarantee your success!

Using your imagination, you can come up with all kinds of ways to integrate wonderful stories into your work with children. Using these tips will guarantee a pleasurable, successful story session every time.

- Select an appropriate story for your listeners.
- Be familiar with the story and the drawing that goes with it.
- Have in mind some ideas for discussion after the story.
- Be ready to hear "Tell it again!"
- Enjoy yourself!

Celebrate life with a story!

Paper-Cutting Directions

What is paper-cutting?

Cutting the "answer" to a story out of a piece of paper is a unique way to tell a story, and it yields an unusual surprise for the listeners. It is also a great way for children to learn to tell stories. The stories are short, easy to learn, and simple to tell.

As you tell these stories, you will be cutting an object out of a piece of paper. At the end of the story, the object is completely cut out. The paper-cutting object is an integral part of the story.

After you tell a few of these stories, your students will soon be telling their own paper-cutting tales both at home and at school. Some children will bring stories to school that they have made up at home; this generates enthusiasm in other children to do the same thing.

Why combine paper-cutting and storytelling?

Telling a story while cutting a piece of paper is a great way to completely capture your listeners' interest.

Watching the object emerge from the paper helps both the storyteller and the listeners remember the steps of the story. The cutting lines are related to the plot, and the object created is important to the outcome of your story.

Another plus: When speaking in front of a group, most people feel more confident if they have something to do with their hands; the paper and scissors fill this need.

Most children love to cut and spend lots of time at it. After experiencing a paper-cutting story involving a simple object, children will often take their own ideas and turn them into a story.

Do you need to be an artist or seasoned storyteller?

No! All you need to do is trace or photocopy! These patterns are designed to be used with any size and color of paper. You do not have to cut freehand; trace your cutting lines lightly before telling the story, or cut on the photocopy lines. Before presenting your story, read it carefully once or twice. Refer back to the story as often as you need to during your telling.

How to tell paper-cutting stories

1. First place a piece of white paper over the pattern in the book. With a pencil, trace cutting lines lightly. Fold where indicated. If you are using

white paper to tell your story, you are ready to go. If you want to transfer the cutting lines to colored paper, cut out your white pattern, place it on the colored paper and trace around it.

Or photocopy the pattern in the book. Cut on the lines. If you wish the cut lines to be less noticeable for listeners, turn the paper over, and cut on the back side of the paper. You will still be able to see the lines, but they will not be obvious to your listeners.

2. Practice telling your story while cutting so that it becomes natural to talk and cut at the same time. Cutting steps are related to the story. As the character goes places or does something, you cut a new line. Becoming familiar with the story and the cutting allows you to present the story easily and develop a natural rapport with your listeners. When you are not cutting, just hold the paper and scissors naturally or put them down if you want to gesture while talking.

If you forget what comes next or get stuck in a story, ask the youngsters to repeat what's happened thus far (giving you time to think) or suggest what could come next.

3. Retell the story at least once. You can involve the listeners by giving them each a photocopy of the drawing and letting them cut and/or color the story as you retell it together. In addition to learning that number or shape, retelling the story gives the listener a second chance to enjoy it. Stories can and should be changed by each storyteller, and a story will be a little bit different each time it is told.

4. After telling the story, help your listeners decide on a good title for it.

How you and your students can create original paper-cutting stories

1. Decide on a story to tell. Then choose something to paper-cut that is an integral part of the story. Or first choose an object to cut, then find a story or create a story involving that object. The easiest objects to draw and cut out are symmetrical. How to Draw books (available in most libraries) are a great resource for ideas.

2. Students should prefold their paper and with a pencil, lightly draw one half of their symmetrical object against the folded side. Older students can make notes about their story, outline their story or even write out their entire story. Remind them to relate their cutting steps to their story line. As their character goes places or does things, they can make their next cut.

3. There are countless variations of paper-cutting. You can fold a differently colored paper inside as in "Two" and "Circle." You can fan-fold your paper as in "Oval." You can weave your paper as in "Square." You and your students will be surprised at how creative you can be with this paper-cutting concept.

4. Expect simple, imperfect cut-outs and stories. Students' stories might even be remarkably similar to one that you have just told. That's okay and quite a compliment to you. You might need to encourage a reluctant child who "just can't think of anything." Help him get ideas from pictures on classroom or library bulletin boards, on classmates' clothing, or on notebooks. Get the child started by asking questions such as, "What else does this outline of a snowman make you think of? Does it look like path? Are some kids walking down this path when they get lost?" (indicate outline of snowman).

5. Have scissors and several sheets of paper for each student. Encourage them to practice telling their story to themselves first and then to a friend. Students may prefer to work together—one friend cuts while the other tells the story.

6. After several practices with small groups over a period of several days, your storytellers will be ready to present their stories to the rest of the group. After their presentations, you might want to present each child with a "Storytelling Certificate" or another story told by you.

Circle

Let's talk about rabbits. You probably know a lot about them, don't you? First of all, what is the most noticeable thing about rabbits? Yes, they have unusually big ears, don't they? **(Cut from 1 to 2, ear.)** These ears help them to hear very well.

What do rabbits eat? Yes, they eat lettuce leaves, radishes, flowers, and lots of other plants. Their stomachs feel especially good when they eat a big lunch of carrots. This makes their stomachs big and round. **(Cut from 2 to 3.)**

But, speaking of lunch, can you think of some animals who would love to catch a rabbit for lunch? Yes, cats, hawks and foxes all try to catch rabbits. Their big, long feet help them run away from these animals. **(Cut from 3 to 4, foot.)**

What color are the rabbits you see in your yard? Yes, that's right. Most are brown. This is so they can blend in with their surroundings, and not be seen. **(Open out and show brown rabbit.)**

So, rabbits today have big ears. **(Point to ears.)** Rabbits stuff their stomachs full of plants for lunch. **(Point to stomach.)** Many rabbits today are brown, and use their feet to run away from foxes and other animals. **(Point to feet.)**

But did you know that a long time ago every single rabbit was white? **(Turn rabbit around to show white rabbit.)**

Rabbits also ate more than just plants and they were best friends with foxes. How did all this change?

Here's the story —

Far ago, Rabbit and Fox did everything together. They took walks together, they went swimming together, and they camped out under the stars together. Everywhere that Rabbit and Fox went, all of their friends always said, "Rabbit, how beautiful your white fur is! How soft and lovely it looks. How do you keep it so white? What is your secret?"

How did Rabbit get white fur? No other animal had white fur. Well, Rabbit would never tell his secret about his white fur.

After a while, Fox became very jealous of Rabbit's beautiful white fur and all the attention Rabbit got for it. No one ever noticed Fox's pretty red fur. No one noticed Fox at all when he was with Rabbit.

Every day Fox said, "Rabbit, I am your best friend. We do everything together. Surely, you can share the secret of your white fur with me. I won't tell anyone else. Come on Rabbit, tell me your secret."

Finally, Rabbit got so tired of Fox asking that he decided to tell Fox his secret. And after all, Fox was Rabbit's best friend. Rabbit whispered in Fox's ear, "I will tell you my secret for white fur, but you must promise never to tell anyone else. Do you promise, Fox?"

Fox said, "Yes, I promise. I will never tell anyone else. What is your secret?"

Rabbit showed Fox his secret. Rabbit pulled a big bag of marshmallows out of his pocket. **(Show a bag of marshmallows to listeners.)**

Fox said, "What? A bag of marshmallows? How can that be your secret to white fur?"

Rabbit put the bag of marshmallows back in his pocket and answered, "Yes, white fur is that easy. Everyday, I eat just one marshmallow and my fur stays as white as snow. Now, remember Fox, you promised that you will not tell anyone else. Fox, are you remembering that you are my best friend? Are you listening to me?"

But Fox was not listening to Rabbit. Fox was not remembering that Rabbit was his best friend. No, Fox was busy thinking of a plan.

Do you know what Fox was planning? Yes, Fox was thinking of a plan to get the bag of marshmallows. Do you know why? Yes, if Fox could only get Rabbit's marshmallows, then Fox himself could eat the marshmallows and his fur would become a beautiful white color. Finally, everyone would notice Fox and not Rabbit.

Fox started sneaking around and following Rabbit. Fox wondered if Rabbit would ever take the bag of marshmallows out of his pocket. Then he wondered—What did Rabbit do with the marshmallows when he went swimming? Where did he hide them then?

Fox had an idea. He said to Rabbit, "Dear friend, it is so hot today, let's go for a swim."

Rabbit said, "Good idea, Fox. I'll be right back." And Rabbit went off to hide his bag of marshmallows.

Fox said, "Okay, Rabbit. I will wait right here by the water for you." But Fox did not wait by the water. Do you know what he did? Yes, he followed Rabbit very quietly and saw where Rabbit hid his marshmallows. Then Fox raced back to the water's edge before Rabbit returned.

They both dove into the cool water. After splashing around for a bit, Fox said, "Rabbit, would you like me to go get us a snack? All of this swimming has made me hungry. I'll be right back."

Rabbit waited for Fox to come back. What do you think Fox did? Did he really go to get a snack? No, Fox raced back to the hiding place and grabbed Rabbit's bag of marshmallows.

As soon as he had the bag in his paws, Fox wanted to eat all the marshmallows right away so that his fur would turn white. But he realized that then Rabbit would know that he had stolen the marshmallows. So Fox decided to wait a few days before eating any. He put the entire bag of marshmallows in a new hiding place and ran back to Rabbit.

Rabbit said, "What took you so long, Fox? What did you bring for us to eat? I'm starving!"

Fox answered, "Oh, I forgot about the snack … uh … I mean I couldn't find anything to eat. Let's just go home."

Over the next few days Rabbit seemed upset. He also did not seem as glossy white as he normally was. In fact, his ears had already begun to turn brown. **(Cut off white ears to show brown ears at 5.)**

The following day Fox said, "Hey there, Rabbit. Have you been walking in the mud? Your feet are all brown." **(Cut off white feet to show brown feet at 6.)** Rabbit did not answer.

A few days later, Fox said to Rabbit, "Rabbit, you must have forgotten to wash your face this morning. It is all brown and dirty." **(Cut off white face to show brown face at 7.)**

Rabbit said, "Fox, my face isn't dirty and I have not been walking in the mud. Since you are my best friend I must tell you—I lost my bag of marshmallows. I am slowly turning brown. What shall I do? Have you seen my bag of marshmallows anywhere? I only have two left, which I found stuck in the bottom of my pocket." At that moment, Rabbit looked down and realized he had turned completely brown. **(Remove white stomach to show all brown rabbit.)**

Fox lied saying, "No, I haven't seen your bag of marshmallows. Why don't you let me hold your last marshmallows for you? You don't want to lose them, too. Here, give them to me!"

Fox started to grab for them. All of a sudden Rabbit realized what must have happened. He yelled, "Fox, did you steal my bag of marshmallows? You did, didn't you? And you were supposed to be my best friend! Give me back my bag of marshmallows."

Fox said, "I can't give you back your bag of marshmallows, Rabbit."

Rabbit asked, "Why not, Fox?"

Fox answered, "Because I can't remember where I hid the bag after I stole it from you, and I have looked everywhere. You, Rabbit, have the only two marshmallows left. Now give them to me!"

Fox reached again for Rabbit's last marshmallows. But Rabbit was too quick for Fox. Rabbit whipped the marshmallows behind his back. **(Swing the marshmallows behind your back.)**

Fox reached around Rabbit for the marshmallows. But Rabbit quickly pulled one from behind him and threw it up into the sky. Now, you know how sticky a marshmallow can be. Rabbit threw that marshmallow so hard that it stuck up there in the sky.

Then, as Rabbit turned and dashed away from Fox, Fox noticed that the other sticky marshmallow was still stuck to Rabbit's backside. So Fox started to chase him, yelling, "Rabbit, come back here with that marshmallow. I want it!"

Today, what do we call that little bit of white on the back of Rabbit? Yes, we call it his cottontail. A rabbit's tail is white but the rest of him is brown, isn't it? **(Place white rabbit head on brown rabbit as cottontail.)** Do you think a rabbit's white tail is really that last marshmallow? Foxes are always chasing rabbits, aren't they? Why? They want that last marshmallow!

What about the other marshmallow that Rabbit threw in the sky? What do we call it? Yes, that's right. We call it the moon. And that's why the moon is in the sky today. **(Hold up white circle of rabbit's stomach to represent the moon.)**

⭐ Activities

1. Discuss the shape of the ends of a marshmallow. Name some other circles in the room. People often wear circles like buttons, hats, rings, bracelets, earrings, necklaces, watches, overall snaps, and shoe decorations.

2. Let everyone eat Rabbit's marshmallows! Perhaps the children would enjoy bringing in other circle foods from home to share with their classmates.

3. Put a large piece of paper on the table or floor and let every child draw circles of all sizes on it.

4. Get out some bubbles and enjoy these circles!

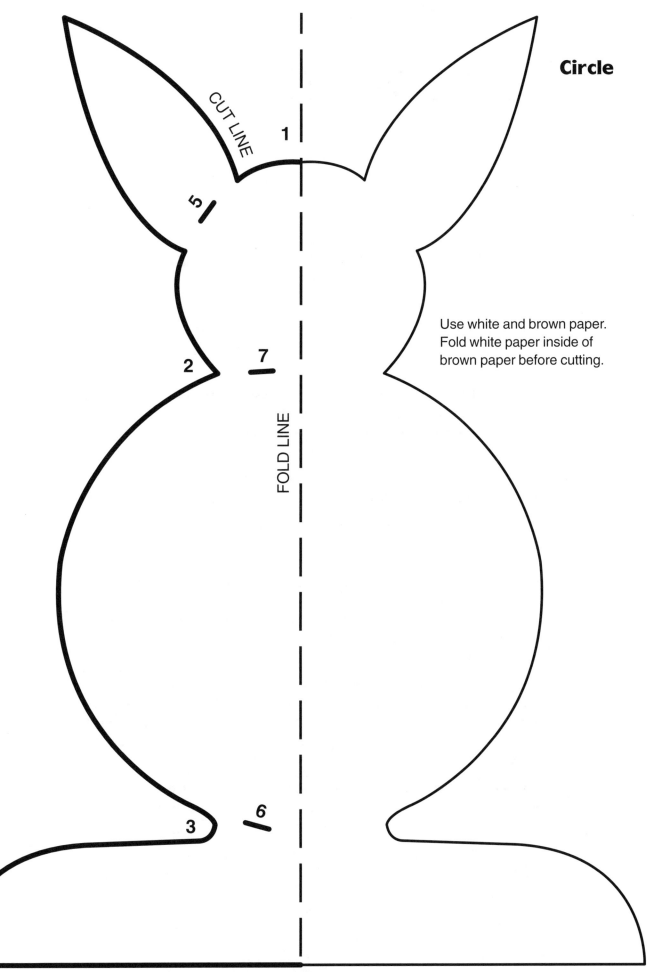

Circle

CUT LINE

1

5

2

7

FOLD LINE

Use white and brown paper.
Fold white paper inside of
brown paper before cutting.

3

6

4

Diamond

For years, everyone had heard the stories about old Mr. Murdock. No one really believed them, but everyone was careful. They say that if Mr. Murdock caught you on his land, he would make you clean all the cages of the snakes he kept in his backyard.

Now, Mr. Murdock was such a strange old man. Because he always grumped at everyone, no one ever went near his land—no one that is except Jubel. Jubel often trespassed on Mr. Murdock's land, but hadn't been caught—not yet, any way.

Jubel knew it was wrong, but he would trespass to steal wood. Every year on Christmas Day, Jubel told himself, "I will not steal wood from Mr. Murdock anymore. I promise myself that I won't do it ever again."

Why did Jubel make this promise to himself on Christmas Day? Because that was when Jubel always gave his mother a beautiful diamond to add to her diamond necklace. **(Cut diamond from prefolded paper.)** Jubel had given his mother a Christmas diamond every year for four years in a row.

Where did Jubel get the money to buy the diamond? He sold the wood that he took from Mr. Murdock's land.

Jubel's mother loved her diamond necklace. She loved it because it was a gift from Jubel. Each Christmas he gave her another diamond to add to her necklace. She wore her necklace every day, and every time she would touch the stones she would think about her loving son. **(Slowly unfold diamonds.)** Jubel's mother always wondered how Jubel had enough money to buy her a diamond every year. But she knew he was a hard worker and saved his money. She would not have been happy if she had known how he had really gotten the money, would she?

One day Jubel did not come home for supper at his usual time. Jubel's mother began to get worried. It was not like Jubel to be late and not let her know. As evening turned into night, Jubel's mother decided to go and look for him. She asked friends in town if they had seen Jubel. No one had seen him, but then someone said, "You might ask old Mr. Murdock about Jubel."

Jubel's mom went up to Mr. Murdock's place. Mr. Murdock took forever to answer his door—or at least it seemed that way. He was even more unfriendly than she remembered. "What do you want?" he growled.

Jubel's mother had a feeling that Jubel was there so she said, "I am here for my son, please."

Mr. Murdock said, "Your son is a thief. I caught him stealing wood from my land this evening."

Jubel's mother was very surprised and said, "I am sorry Mr. Murdock. He shouldn't have done that. May I please talk to him?"

She followed Mr. Murdock to his backyard. She saw hundreds of snakes in cages all around. Then she saw Jubel. He was cleaning out one of the snake cages.

"Jubel!" she cried. "Did you take Mr. Murdock's wood? Why?"

Jubel answered, "I wanted to give you something nice for Christmas and I didn't have any money."

His mother replied, "Oh Jubel, you don't have to buy me something fancy to show me you love me."

Then Mr. Murdock said with a mean smile, "You or Jubel will have to pay me. Of course, if you would rather clean out all of my snake cages every day for the rest of your life, I would not mind. Too bad all of my snakes are poisonous."

Jubel's mother looked at the snakes in their cages. She saw their sharp fangs. Her fingers touched her necklace. Quickly, she took off her necklace and held it in her hand. She said, "Here, take my necklace! We are leaving!"

Mr. Murdock laughed a mean laugh, and stretched out a grimy hand for the diamond necklace. All of the sudden, Jubel's mother threw the necklace at him. Mr. Murdock ducked and the necklace landed in a snake cage behind him. He turned around to grab the necklace out of the cage. But before he could reach it, the snake opened his mouth and swallowed the necklace.

Mr. Murdock opened the cage and carefully took the snake out, holding it so that it could not bite him. He yelled to the snake, "Give me back that necklace!" He squeezed the snake so hard that Jubel could see the outline of the necklace along the snake's back. But the snake still did not cough up the necklace.

Then Mr. Murdock shook the snake to try and get diamond necklace. He shook the snake so hard that you could hear the necklace rattle inside the snake. But the snake still did not cough up the necklace.

Mr. Murdock was still squeezing and shaking the snake as Jubel and his mother ran home. Jubel never stole anything again, and Mr. Murdock never did get that necklace out of the snake.

Today there is a certain type of snake called the Diamondback Rattlesnake. You can still see the outline of the diamond necklace on its back. When this snake gets angry, he shakes. That's when you can hear the necklace rattling inside his tail. **(Show diamond necklace again.)**

✏️✨ Activities

1. Discuss Jubel's actions and the consequences of them. Is it right to steal something from someone else if you think it is for a good reason? How else might Jubel have gotten the money for a present for his mother? Could he have gotten her something else less expensive?

2. With your listeners, discuss the shape of diamonds. Point out that they are made out of two triangles.

3. What other types of diamonds are there in addition to those used in jewelry? Baseball diamonds, diamonds used in factory tools to cut metal.

4. Give each child some clay or Play-Doh. Encourage them to roll the clay between their hands to make long thin rolls or they can roll the clay back and forth on the table to make a long thin snake. You might want to provide some nonfiction books on rattlesnakes. Perhaps there are pictures of diamondback rattlesnakes in one of the books.

Diamond

Use yellow or goldenrod paper.

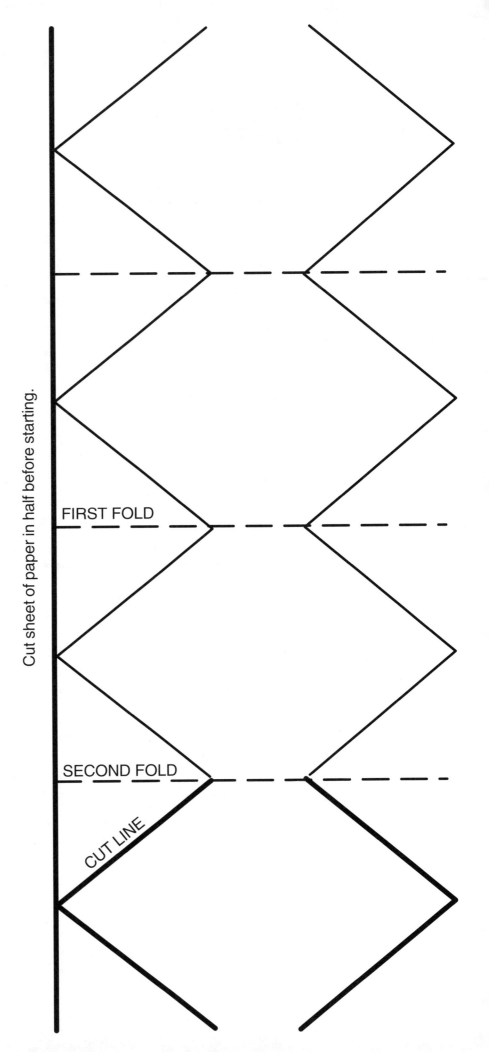

Cut sheet of paper in half before starting.

FIRST FOLD

SECOND FOLD

CUT LINE

Heart

Do you know where your heart is? Yes, it's right here. (**Point to your heart.**) We all know that people have hearts and animals have hearts.

When you go to the doctor, she listens to your heartbeat, doesn't she? How does she do that? Yes, the doctor has a stethoscope, a special instrument that helps her hear your heart.

Your heart is one of the most important parts of your body. I bet you already knew that. But did you know that your heart is a muscle? It is a busy muscle that works all the time. It pumps blood to all parts of your body—from the top of your head to the bottom of your feet.

Many people think that your heart is shaped like this. (**Cut out big heart, 1 to 2.**) But it is not shaped exactly like this, it's really shaped more like your fist. Your heart is actually hollow. Blood flows in on one side through your veins, and the heart muscle squeezes it out on the other side through your arteries.

How big is your heart? Here is an easy way to tell. Make a fist with your hand. Your heart is about the same size as your fist. When you were a baby, your heart was very small. (**Cut our small heart, 3 to 4.**)

As you grow bigger, your heart grows bigger. Now that you are older, your heart is bigger. (**Cut out middle size heart, 5 to 6.**)

How can we feel our own hearts beating? Put two of your fingers on the side of your neck. Can you feel your heartbeat? Notice how fast it is beating now. Have you noticed that sometimes your heart beats very slowly and sometimes it beats very fast? Let's see if we can change how fast our hearts are beating by running in place. Run as fast as you can until I say stop. Then we will stop and see how fast our hearts are beating after we exercise. (**Run in place to count of 10.**)

Now, let's all lay down and rest. (**Everyone rests on floor for 30 seconds.**) As we rest, our heart does not beat as fast. Can you feel your heart slowing down? When you are resting, your heart slows down because it does not need to pump as much blood to your arms and legs.

As you go about your daily activities of work and play, your heart beats about 90 times a minute. When you run around on the playground, your heart beats faster. When you go to sleep at night, your heart beats more slowly.

How can we take good care of our hearts? There are several things that we can do. First, we can get enough sleep every night. Second, we can eat foods that will help our hearts grow healthy and strong. Third, exercising helps our hearts stay healthy.

Perhaps you can share some of these interesting heart facts with your mom and dad or grandma and grandpa, and then show them how to cut a heart out of paper.

Activities

1. Photocopy the heart pattern on the next page in a variety of colors. Give each child a copy. Show them how to fold their paper down the middle. Let them cut the hearts out with you as you review some of the facts in the story. At the end of the story, encourage children to trade a heart with their friend so that they all have hearts of different colors. Use the cut out hearts to make an art project.

2. Have a variety of sizes and colors of hearts already cut out. Invite the children to create a picture of an animal or object using the hearts.

3. Cut small to large hearts out of heavy cardboard. Use masking tape to secure the hearts to the table. Encourage children to place a piece of paper over the hearts to make a rubbing with a crayon.

4. Trifold a piece of paper. In each section, encourage the children to draw a picture of themselves doing an activity to help their heart grow—sleeping, eating good foods, or exercising.

   Use a heart sticker or glue a small cutout heart on the pictures the children draw of themselves.

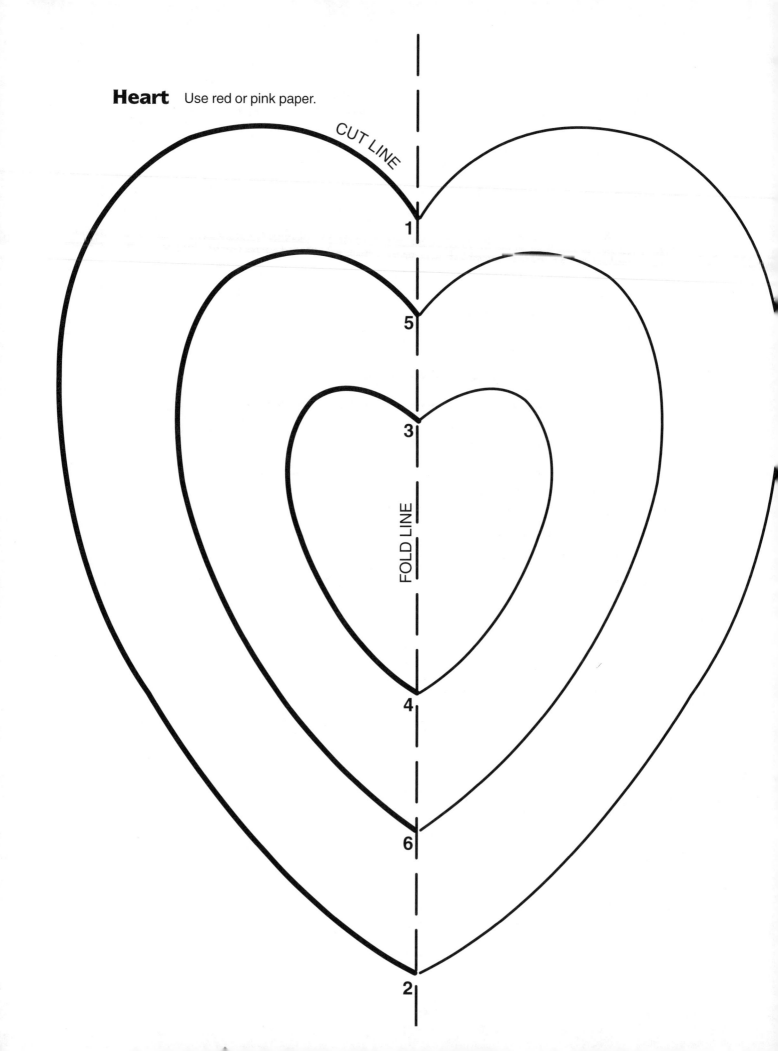

Heart Use red or pink paper.

CUT LINE

FOLD LINE

1

5

3

4

6

2

Oval

What shape are most eggs? Yes, they are ovals. Let's name some creatures that lay eggs. Yes, birds, turtles, snakes, alligators and insects all lay eggs. Insects probably lay the most eggs because there are more insects than any other living creature in the world. Most insect eggs are oval. **(Fold paper at fold lines as numbered.)**

What do you think is the prettiest insect in the world? Yes, many people think that it is a butterfly. Butterflies live all over the world, in jungles, swamps, deserts, forests, backyards and school playgrounds. The smallest butterfly is about the size of your fingernail and the biggest butterfly in the world is bigger than your hand. Scientists have identified thousands of different kinds of butterflies, and still each one is unique, just like each of us is unique.

Everyone loves the bright colors and silent zig-zag flight of the butterfly. Many people think that if a butterfly lands on you, then you will have good luck.

What shape do you think the egg of a butterfly is? Yes, it is an oval. **(Cut paper and display oval. Do not unfold.)** Here is our egg.

Every butterfly starts out life as an egg. But in just a short time, the egg hatches and a tiny caterpillar or larva emerges. **(Fold egg in half to create tiny half oval larva.)**

This tiny caterpillar has only one job and that is to eat and eat and eat! First the caterpillar eats the leaf that it is sitting on. Then, it crawls to the next leaf on the plant or onto another plant to find more leaves to eat. A caterpillar has strong jaws for chewing leaves. All this eating makes the caterpillar grow bigger and bigger and bigger. **(Open out the paper one section at a time as you are talking.)**

After a few weeks of eating and growing, the caterpillar is ready for a big change. The caterpillar settles down on a tree branch to spin a cocoon or chrysalis around itself. **(Refold paper to one oval and let this represent a cocoon.)**

From the outside, it looks as if nothing is happening. But inside, great changes are taking place. The caterpillar is busy changing into a butterfly. It grows wings, six long legs, antennae and a mouth that can drink but not eat. Soon a full-size butterfly emerges with two beautiful wings. **(Open out to two sections to represent butterfly.)**

The butterfly's wing colors and patterns are very important because this helps it survive. Some butterflies have soft colors that help them blend in with their surroundings. Others have very bright colors that warn birds that they do not taste very good. Still others are not harmful to birds but look almost exactly like other butterflies that are harmful. Some butterflies have two large spots on their wings that look like eyes. These help scare away birds.

Butterflies usually only live for a few short weeks. Then they find a mate and lay eggs so that a new cycle of butterflies may begin.

Butterflies are beautiful and fascinating creatures to watch. The next time that you see a butterfly, notice its delicate design and the dancing flight. And look for all of those ovals in the butterfly's body and wing designs.

Activities

1. Use ink pad and thumbprints to retell the story. One thumbprint can be the egg. Several thumbprints lined up can represent a caterpillar. One thumbprint in the middle and two at an angle on each side can be the butterfly. Add legs and antennae with felt-tip marker.

2. Let children color with markers on coffee filters. Use a spray bottle to spray lightly with water. The water helps the colors mix into beautiful colors and shapes. When the coffee filter is dry, squeeze the middle together and twist with a pipe cleaner. Let the ends of the pipe cleaner stick out to be the antennae. Glue onto a clothespin. Add a piece of magnetic tape to the back to make a great butterfly refrigerator magnet.

3. Can you name some foods that are shaped like an oval? The first one that you might think of is an egg. But there are oval-shaped crackers, grapes, little hot dogs, olives, avocados, potatoes, small carrots, and onions.

4. Cut white paper into butterfly shape. Using a Q-tip, put splotches of bright color on one wing only. Then press the paper together, transferring the paint from one wing to the next.

Oval

Use yellow paper.

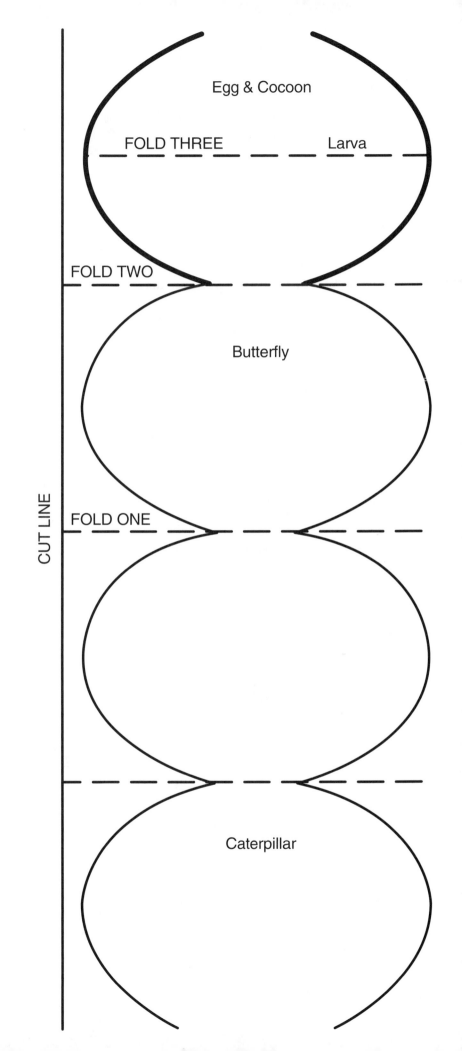

Egg & Cocoon

FOLD THREE — — — — Larva

FOLD TWO — — — —

Butterfly

FOLD ONE — — — —

CUT LINE

Caterpillar

Rectangle

Have you ever wondered why pigs are called pigs? If you call someone a pig you are really insulting them, aren't you?

It did not use to be this way. Many years ago, it was considered a great compliment if someone called you a pig. How did being called a pig change from a good thing to a bad thing? Here's the story —

Far ago pigs had the best manners in the world. They were known for the polite way in which they behaved. Pigs sat daintily at their dining room tables. They carefully ate with their knives and forks and spoons. They always used their napkins to wipe the food off of their mouths. At the end of the day, pigs took baths with perfumed soap. While they were soaking in their scented bubblebaths, they would read their cookbooks and decide what to cook for their next delicious meal.

But then, almost overnight, one pig changed all this.

This particular pig really, really loved taking a nice long bath before bedtime. **(Cut from 1 to 2.)** Here is Pig's bathtub. What shape is it? Yes, that's correct. It is a rectangle. Is your bathtub shaped like a rectangle?

Pig loved eating at his table. **(Cut from 3 to 4.)** Here is Pig's table. What shape is this? Yes, it's a rectangle, too.

Pig loved reading recipes from cookbooks. He loved making fabulous, fancy foods to eat. **(Cut from 5 to 6. Fold paper in half to represent a book.)** Here is Pig's cookbook. What shape is this? Yes, it's another rectangle.

Pig used nice cloth napkins to wipe the food from his face. **(Show other rectangle.)** Here is one of Pig's napkins. I bet you know what shape this is— another rectangle.

Pig was getting tired of his same old dining room table, his same cloth napkin, his same old cookbook and his same old bathtub. He started wondering if eating a fancy meal at someone else's dinner table would be more fun than at his own. He wondered if using someone else's napkin and taking a bath in someone else's bathtub would also be more fun. Pig decided to find out. He got rid of his old bathtub, table, napkin and cookbook. **(Wad up 4 cut rectangles and toss over shoulder.)** It was time for new ones. But where would he get them?

Pig came up with a plan. He decided to "borrow" these things from his friends.

First, Pig visited his friend Bear and brought him some taffy apples. After Pig and Bear enjoyed their sticky snack right down to the last bite, Pig said, "Do you mind if I use your bathroom to wash up a bit? That taffy apple made my hands very sticky."

Soon Pig came out of the bathroom. He said, "Bear, while I was washing my hands, I noticed that your bathtub really needs painting. It's all scratched. If you help me carry it to my house, I will repaint it for you. I have just the color that will match your bathroom." **(Use a second piece of paper, of a different color. Cut a new bathtub from 1 to 2.)**

Bear was very grateful. He agreed and helped carry his bathtub over to Pig's house. Do you think that Pig is really going to repaint the bathtub? No, of course not. Pig was tricking Bear, wasn't he?

Next, Pig decided to visit his friend Deer. He said, "Look Deer, I brought you this great jigsaw puzzle. Would you like to put it together with me?"

Pig and Deer started on the puzzle on Deer's dining room table. Then Pig said, "Deer, have you noticed how scratched your table is? If you help me carry it to my house, I will be happy to sand down the scratches and refinish your table for you." **(Cut a table from the second piece of paper, from 3 to 4.)**

What do you think Deer said? That's right. Deer agreed and helped carry his table over to Pig's house. Do you think that Pig is really going to refinish Deer's table? No, of course not. Pig was tricking Deer, wasn't he?

The following day, Pig took some nice juicy ears of corn to Raccoon. Pig knew that corn was Raccoon's favorite food. You know how messy corn on the cob is. Raccoon and Pig used all of Raccoon's best cloth napkins. After they finished eating all the corn, Pig said, "Raccoon, I will be happy to take these dirty napkins home and wash them for you." **(Cut remaining rectangle in half, 5 to 6, for the napkins.)**

What do you think Raccoon said? Yes, Raccoon gratefully agreed and gave Pig all of his napkins to take home with him. Do you think that Pig is really going to wash Raccoon's napkins and give them back to him? No, of course not. Pig was tricking Raccoon, wasn't he?

Do you remember that Pig also wanted a new cookbook? So Pig went over to Goat's house and said, "Goat, I know that you are a rather picky eater and will not eat just anything. I thought that you might like to try out some special recipes. I can write some new ones down for you." **(Fold last remaining rectangle in half for a cookbook.)**

Pig sat down at Goat's table and started writing. But after awhile he said, "You know, Goat, this is taking a rather long time. I think that it would be easier if I took your cookbook home with me and wrote the recipes directly into your book for you. Would you mind?"

What do you think Goat said? You are correct. Goat graciously let Pig take home his recipe book. Do you think that Pig is really going to give Goat some new recipes? No, of course not. Pig was tricking Goat, wasn't he?

Days went by. Weeks went by. Pig did not return Bear's bathtub. **(Show bathtub.)** He did not return Deer's table. **(Show table.)** Pig did not give Raccoon back his napkins. **(Show napkins.)** He also never returned Goat's cookbook. **(Show cookbook.)**

Pig's friends were very unhappy with him. They asked him each day to return their things. Each day Pig made some excuse and promised to return the bathtub, table, napkin and cookbook tomorrow.

Finally, all the friends asked Coyote to give Pig a visit and get their things back for them. Coyote carried a big package to Pig's house. He knocked on the door. When Pig came to the door, Coyote said, "Good morning, Pig. I brought you some cookies. May I put them on your dining room table?"

Without waiting for an answer, Coyote marched right into Pig's house and straight into the dining room. Coyote set his big package down on Deer's table and began to unwrap it. Pig's eyes got very big because inside was the biggest plate of cookies Pig had ever seen.

Then, Coyote did something that Pig did not expect. Coyote threw the huge plate of cookies out Pig's dining room window! Cookies went flying everywhere! What do you think Pig did? Yes, he ran outside and began picking up the cookies. Actually, Pig only picked up a few cookies before he sat down to eat them right there in the yard. That was exactly what Coyote wanted Pig to do.

Do you know what Coyote did while Pig was outside eating cookies? He quickly searched through Pig's house. He found Goat's cookbook and Raccoon's napkins and put them on the table. But, could he carry both the bathtub and table all by himself? No.

Coyote was prepared for this problem. Along with the package of cookies, Coyote had also brought a very sharp saw! Do you know what Coyote did with that saw? Yes, he sawed Bear's bathtub and Deer's table in half. What Coyote did not know, was that while he was sawing the table in half, he accidentally sawed the cookbook and napkins in half also. **(Stack papers, then cut them in half.)** But, oh well, at least everything was now small enough for Coyote to carry by himself. Coyote carried everything out of Pig's house while Pig was still outside eating cookies.

Deer, Bear, Raccoon and Goat were anxiously waiting for Coyote when he arrived home. Coyote said, "Friends, I did great! I distracted Pig and got all of your things back for you. I had to saw them in half to carry them, but here they are!"

Bear looked at the two pieces of his bathtub. He said, "Coyote, you sawed my bathtub in half! Now I can never take a bath!" This is why bears to this very day always smell so badly—they never take baths—they can't because Coyote sawed their bathtub in half. **(Show two pieces of tub.)** Are the two pieces of bathtub still rectangles?

Deer looked at his table and said, "Coyote, you sawed my table in half? Now I can never eat sitting down!" This is why deer to this very day eat standing up—they don't have a table because Coyote sawed it in half. (**Show two pieces of table.**) Are the two pieces of table still rectangles?

Raccoon looked at his napkins and said, "Coyote, you sawed my napkins in half. How can I use them now!" This is why raccoons to this very day wash their paws in water. They don't have any napkins, thanks to Coyote. (**Show two pieces of napkin.**) Are the two pieces of napkin still rectangles?

Goat looked at his cookbook and said, "Coyote, you sawed my cookbook in half. How can I even read any of my special recipes?"

This is why goats today eat anything and everything. (**Show two pieces of cookbook.**) Are the two pieces of cookbook still rectangles?

All of the animals yelled, "Coyote, you ruined everything. You're not our friend anymore!"

What happened to Coyote? His friends were all so mad at him that they never spoke to him again. And that's why Coyotes don't not have any friends today.

What about Pig? He also no longer had a bathtub. He no longer had a table to eat on, or napkins to wipe his mouth with. Plus, he did not have a cookbook. So what did he do? What do pigs do today? You know what they don't do. Pigs don't take baths. They don't use napkins. Pigs eat their food while standing in it, and they don't care what they eat. That's why being called a pig is no longer such a nice thing.

☄ Activities

1. Let the children retell the story with you and cut out their own bathtub, table, napkin and cookbook.

2. Ask children to name some rectangles that are in the classroom, such as a book, door, table, mirror.

3. Encourage each child to create an original picture using rectangles in a variety of sizes.

4. Present children with a wide range of rectangles of all different sizes. Ask them to put the rectangles in order of smallest to largest.

5. This is a very silly explanation of why bears don't take baths, goats eat anything, etc. Discuss other animals and create a silly explanation for one of their behaviors.

Rectangle

Make two photocopies; on
on white paper and one on
a second color.

Bathtub

Napkin

Table

Book   FOLD LINE

Square

Far ago, when the world was new, there was a thief. But this thief did not steal gold, jewels or money. No, this thief enjoyed taking very unusual things—he loved to collect interesting shapes. Do you know who this thief was? It was Raccoon!

The first shape that Raccoon decided to steal was the circle. He took all the circles that he could find, and put them in places where the other animals could never get them. He put the circles on sunflowers, raindrops, and lily pads. Can you think of some other places where Raccoon hid circles?

Raccoon even hid some circles on himself. Do you know where? Yes, he hid some of the circles around his eyes and on his tail, didn't he?

The animals were very upset but Raccoon laughed and said, "Ha, ha. I stole all the circles and now I am planning to steal another shape. Do you know what shape is next? It is the square! Actually, I have already stolen all the squares and hidden them in one of my hollow trees. Tonight, while you are all sleeping, I will put the squares where you can not get them back, just like I did with the circles."

The animals asked each other, "What can we do about our squares?"

Spider spoke up, "Raccoon has our squares. But I can make some new ones. Tonight while he is hiding our squares, I will make some new ones."

The animals asked, "But how, Spider? Raccoon said that he has all the squares. How can you make new ones?"

Spider answered, "Here, look at these rectangles." **(Show black strips of paper.)**

The animals asked, "But what will you do with the rectangles? What does that have to do with squares?"

Spider answered, "I have a plan. Now leave me alone until morning." Spider shut his door and locked it. **(Show red paper rectangle.)**

Spider worked all night. Spider did what he did best. Do you know what spiders do best ? Yes, spiders can weave. They usually use their weaving skills to make webs, but on this particular night Spider was planning to weave something different. All night, Spider wove back and forth, back and forth. **(Weave the black strips into the red paper.)**

In the morning, Spider unlocked and opened his door. Then he carefully carried his weaving outside for everyone to see. All the animals thought Spider's weaving was so beautiful. **(Show weaving.)**

Just then Raccoon walked by. He laughed, "Ha, ha. I have been up all night, hiding all the squares. Now you have no more squares."

Spider said, "But Raccoon, I have been working all night on squares too. Look at this." Spider held up his weaving for Raccoon to see. **(Hold up weaving again.)**

Raccoon looked at Spider's weaving. He said, "That's not a square, that's a rectangle. Don't you even know your shapes, Spider?"

Spider answered, "Look again, Raccoon. Do you see any squares in this rectangle?"

Raccoon looked again more carefully at Spider's weaving. He saw that it was indeed filled with squares. Raccoon was furious! He yelled, "You had better guard your squares carefully, Spider. Because if you ever let them out of your sight, I will steal those squares too."

What do you think this looks like? Yes, this reminds me of a checkerboard.

Spider said, "Don't worry. We will all take turns using our checkerboard. Our squares are safe forever." And they have been.

For as long as there is someone playing checkers somewhere in the world, the squares are safe. Do you think that there is a checker game going on somewhere right now?

But there is one animal who never plays checkers. Do you know who that is? Yes, it is Raccoon. You have never seen a raccoon playing checkers and you never will. This is because the other animals won't let him play checkers and now you know why.

⭐ Activities

1. Ask listeners if they like to play checkers, and when they last played. Hold up a checkerboard and let everyone count how many squares there are on the board.

2. Ask the children if they have ever made a weaving like Spider did. Let everyone have an opportunity to make their own checkerboard. Retell the story after everyone is finished weaving their checkerboard.

3. Bring in a variety of square crackers for the children to eat. Graham crackers are fun to use for this activity because they are packaged as a long rectangle. Show children how graham crackers can be broken in half to form a square and then broken in half again to become two rectangles.

4. For a simple activity with squares, make a photocopy of the checkerboard drawing from this book and let each child color in the squares with markers or crayons.

Square

Weave 2⅛"x 8½" strips of black paper through cut red paper.

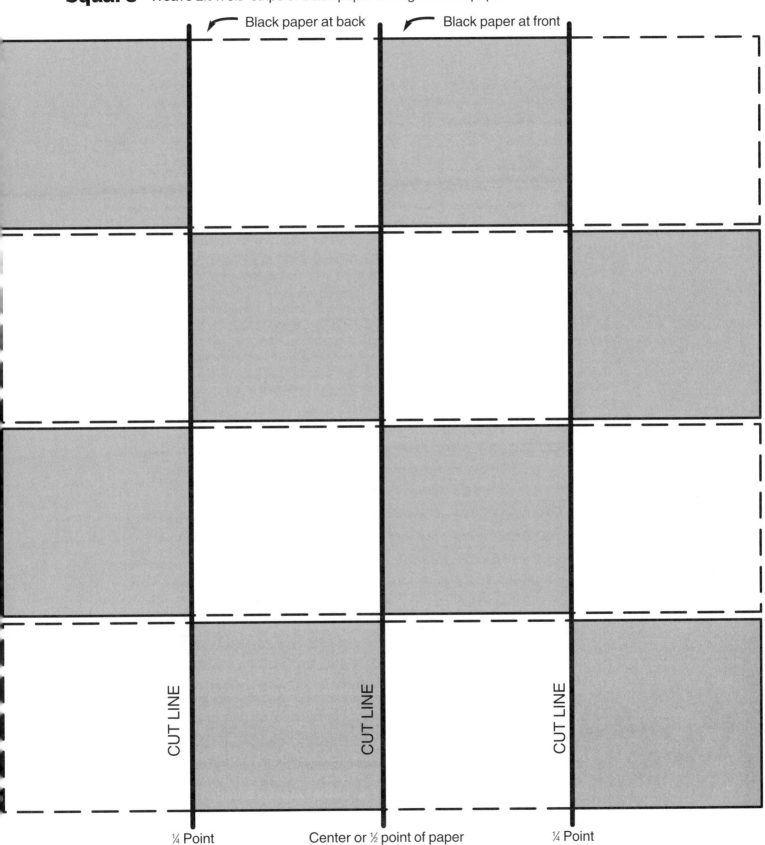

Black paper at back

Black paper at front

CUT LINE

CUT LINE

CUT LINE

¼ Point

Center or ½ point of paper

¼ Point

# Star

Far ago, a poor man was passing through a very small town. He had no job and no money. He was not very smart and so he decided that the easiest way to get money was to steal it. It was a hot afternoon and he was tired, so he decided to sit down to rest. He found a nice shady spot next to a small school building. How do you think he knew it was a school? Yes, he saw the playground.

The school windows were open and he could hear the murmur of voices coming from inside. He was just about to fall asleep when he heard loud voices, "No, I want one. Give me one first. Here teacher! Where is mine?!"

With so many voices calling out to be next, it was obvious to the thief that whatever the teacher was handing out must be very valuable. Cautiously, he raised his head and took a peek through the open window.

Do you know what he saw? He saw a teacher with a stack of papers in her hands. **(Show paper.)** All the students were crowded around her. He heard the teacher say, "Now, wait your turn. Everyone must be patient. Everyone will get one."

As soon as a child had a paper in his hand, he folded it, stuffed it in his book bag, and ran out the door. **(Fold paper into fourths.)** .

The thief thought, "Those papers must be very valuable, if each child is trying so hard to get one and everyone only gets one. Look how they all run away as soon as they get a paper. They must be afraid that someone will steal their paper. I think I should steal those papers."

After resting a while longer, the thief walked over to the grocery. **(Cut from 1 to 2.)** He saw two of the students from the class. One of them seemed upset. "I can't find my paper anywhere," the child moaned.

The thief thought "Someone must have stolen his paper already. The papers must be more valuable than I thought if he is so upset at losing his."

That evening, the thief looked in the window of one of the student's houses. He saw that the child was stuffing his paper under his bed. The thief thought, "That child doesn't want anything to happen to his paper, so he is hiding it."

At the next house, the thief saw a child put a paper on top of his refrigerator. "That is a good hiding place for his paper. Look at all the stuff on top of that refrigerator. No one will ever find it there." **(Cut from 2 to 3.)**

At the street carnival that night, the thief saw the teacher. He overheard her say to several of the children, "If you bring me back your paper, I will give you a star. Please give me back your paper on Monday."

The thief thought, "Now the teacher wants the papers back because she is sorry she gave away such valuable papers. I must find a way to steal those papers."

On Monday morning, the thief hid behind a bush under the open school window. He watched from his hiding place as all the students walked into school. **(Cut from 3 to 4.)**

Then he heard the teacher say, "Okay class, I want all your papers back now please. Remember, anyone who gives me their paper gets a star!"

Some children had excuses as to why they could not give her back their papers. He heard the children say, "I left mine at home. I couldn't find mine. My mom took mine and put it somewhere."

The thief thought, "Wow! They do not want to give up those papers. I will steal them for myself."

The teacher collected the papers. She said, "For all of you who turned in your papers, I will give you a star."

Just as she turned to put the papers on her desk, the thief jumped through the window, ran over to the teacher's desk and grabbed the stack of papers from her hands. Then he ran out the door as fast as he could. **(Cut from 4 to 5.)**

Once again hidden in the bushes, the poor thief looked at the papers that he had stolen. I am quite sure that he was very surprised.

Do you know what kind of papers the thief stole? Yes, he stole the children's homework sheets. What do you think he could do with the homework? Absolutely nothing—except maybe grade them. And if they haven't been returned yet, I guess he's still doing just that.

And where is the star that the teacher gave all of the children who handed in their homework sheets? Why, it is right here. **(Open out paper and show star.)**

⭐ Activities

1. Discuss why the children put their homework under their beds, or on top of their refrigerators. Discuss unusual or funny places that homework papers could end up. Ask them if they or their siblings or friends have ever lost their homework sheets.

2. Discuss why the teacher was going to give the children a star for turning in their homework. Was the star a sticker to be put on their chart? Ask how many children have star charts at home.

3. If available, use a die-cut machine to cut stars in a variety of colors of construction paper, wrapping paper or wallpaper. Punch holes in one point and let children make star necklaces. Glue two stars back to back on a tongue depressor to make a magic wand. Add glitter or other decorations.

4. Discuss different ways to draw a star. Two triangles could be used. A star could be drawn from a letter A.

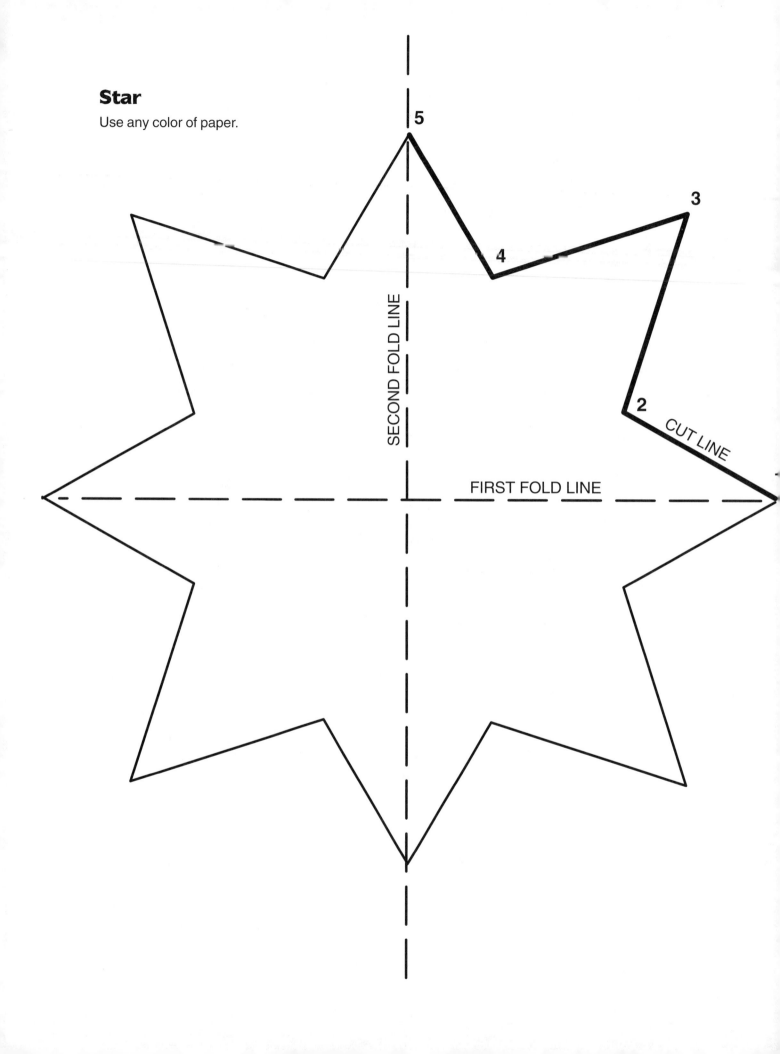

Star

Use any color of paper.

5

3

4

2

SECOND FOLD LINE

CUT LINE

FIRST FOLD LINE

Triangle

Have you ever done something funny—like wear socks that don't match, or put hair gel in your hair so that it sticks up all over? **(Let children share funny things that they have done.)**

One day a friend of mine, Noelle, picked a shape—her favorite shape, and decided that all the food she ate that day had to be in her favorite shape. She said, "Since this is my special day, I will only eat foods in my special shape."

See if you can guess what her favorite shape is. I will give you some hints.

For breakfast, Noelle at a piece of pizza her mom saved from the night before. **(Cut 1 to 2.)** Raise your hand if you have you ever eaten pizza for breakfast.

For lunch, Noelle ate nachos covered with cheese. **(Cut 2 to 3.)**

For a snack, Noelle ate a slice of apple pie. **(Cut 3 to 4.)**

For dinner, Noelle cut her peanut butter sandwich into her special shape, and then she ate it. **(Cut 4 to 5.)**

You know what Noelle's favorite shape is, don't you? Yes, it is a triangle. Let's look closely at this triangle. **(Show one folded cut-out triangle.)** How many sides does a triangle have? How many corners does a triangle have?

Which of these triangle-shaped foods do you like to eat?

On Noelle's special day, she ate only triangular foods. She also wore a special hat, made out of lots of triangles. Do you see all of these triangles? **(Staple or tape ends of sawtooth paper together to make crown.)**

Then Noelle got out her box of markers and decorated her crown with lots of triangles. As she worked, she sang a little song. **(Sing to the tune of "Found a Peanut.")**

> "Lots of markers, lots of markers, lots of markers help me draw.
>   Lots of angles, lots of angles, lots of angles on my paper.
>
>   Lots of angles, lots of angles, lots of angles make for me
>   Lots of triangles, lots of triangles, lots of triangles for my birthday."

It was Noelle's special day because it was her birthday! Here is her birthday crown. Does anyone here have a birthday coming up soon? If you or one of your friends is having a birthday soon, you might want to make a birthday crown. Remember to cut out lots of triangles!

✦ Activities

1. Let everyone make and decorate a crown. Keep things simple by giving each child a photocopy of the crown pattern on the next page. Show them how to fold it and then let them cut it out. Use markers, crayons, glitter, scraps of wrapping paper or construction paper. Staple ends together to fit child's head.

2. Share a snack of triangle foods. This could be a bag of nachos or other triangle-shaped snack chip, pieces of cheese, etc.

3. Give each child a piece of bread. Help them cut the bread diagonally into two triangles. Spread with jelly or peanut butter as desired.

4. Supply Popsicle sticks and glue and encourage children to make triangles. Toothpicks will also make great triangles but are more difficult for young fingers to work with.

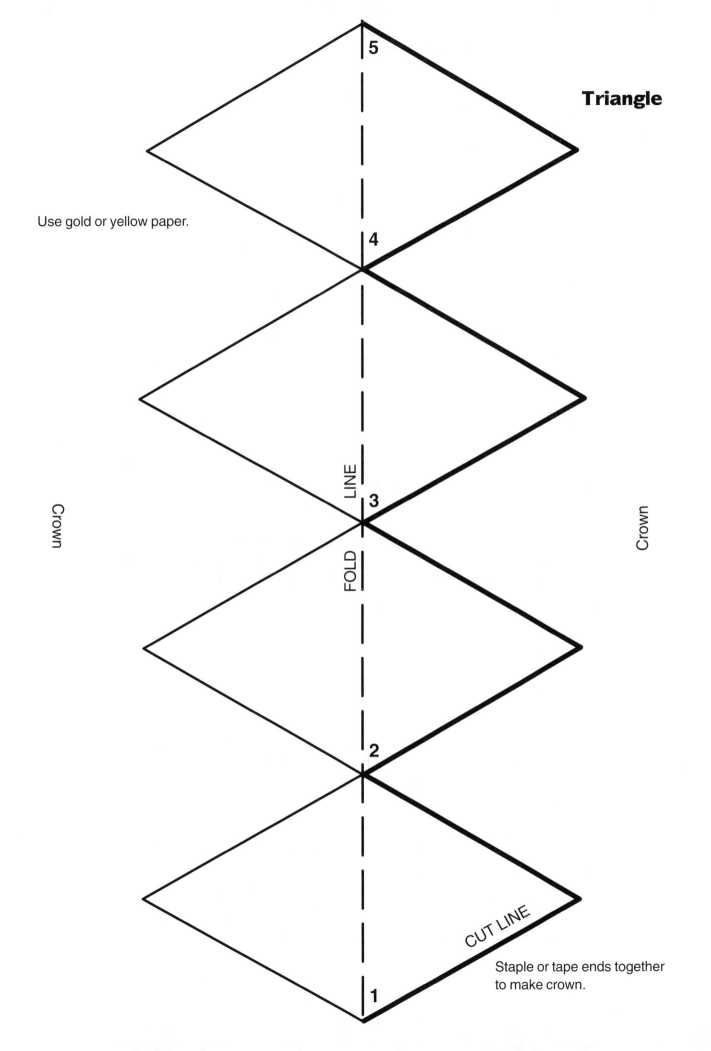

Triangle

Use gold or yellow paper.

5

4

LINE

3

FOLD

Crown

Crown

2

CUT LINE

1

Staple or tape ends together to make crown.

Shapes Review

One fall day, a brother and sister took a walk after school. Let's see, we need a name for this brother and sister. **(Choose names from listeners in the audience.)** Let's use the names Sarah and Charlie. Sarah and Charlie decided to walk to the little pond in their neighborhood. **(Cut half circle on side of paper folded in half for the lake, 1. Show half hole only.)**

Do you know why they went down to the pond? It was because they had made a boat, and they wanted to see if it would float. **(Fold top of paper down to hole. Cut up on both sides of paper to show boat, 2 and 3. Fingers should cover up hole.)**

They put it in the water and it floated—for awhile. After a while the cardboard became wetter and wetter and finally the boat sprang a leak. **(Move fingers away from hole. Show hole.)** Do you see this hole? What shape is it? Yes, that's right, it's a circle.

What do you think happened to Charlie and Sarah's boat? Yes, it sank! It was suppertime anyway so they walked back home. **(Unfold paper and show house.)** You know that there were lots of houses on Charlie and Sarah's street, but the children always knew which house was theirs. It was easy to tell, because you could see Charlie's bedroom window, **(Unfold paper and refold one fourth of the way in. Cut half square, 5.)** and Sarah's bedroom window. **(Unfold paper and refold one fourth of the way in. Cut half square, 6.)** What shape are their windows? Yes, they are squares.

They walked up to their front door and went right in because the door was standing wide open. **(Cut 7 to 8, fold door open.)** What shape is the door? That's right, it's a rectangle.

Charlie said, "Oh, no. If the front door is open, then that means our pet must have gotten out. If she got out, then how will we ever find her?"

Sarah and Charlie looked all around for their pet. **(Fold bottom side of house into triangles.)** Finally they found her. They were so happy.

Do you know what kind of pet Charlie and Sarah had? Yes, it was a … cat. **(Turn house over to show cat.)**

What shape are the ears of the cat? Yes, that is correct. They are triangles. Let's review the rest of our shapes one last time. **(Point to each shape on the house/cat and help the children name each one.)**

Some cats love to stay in the house and never go out. Do you know what they are called? Yes, they are called "house cats." And now you know why, here is our house **(Show house.)** and here is our cat. **(Show cat.)**

✏️✨ Activities

1. Make a boat with the children. There are several easy ways to make a boat. They can use the bottom half of a milk carton, a plastic soda bottle cut lengthwise, or cardboard glued together.

2. Children might like to make their own cat by gluing two small triangles on top of one larger one. They can add yarn or pipecleaner whiskers.

3. To review all the shapes again, give children Play-Doh to create the basic shapes.

4. Challenge the children to use six Popsicle sticks or less to make all of the shapes except the circle. Children can work with a partner to make the shapes. Give the children more Popsicle sticks and let them work together to make one large circle.

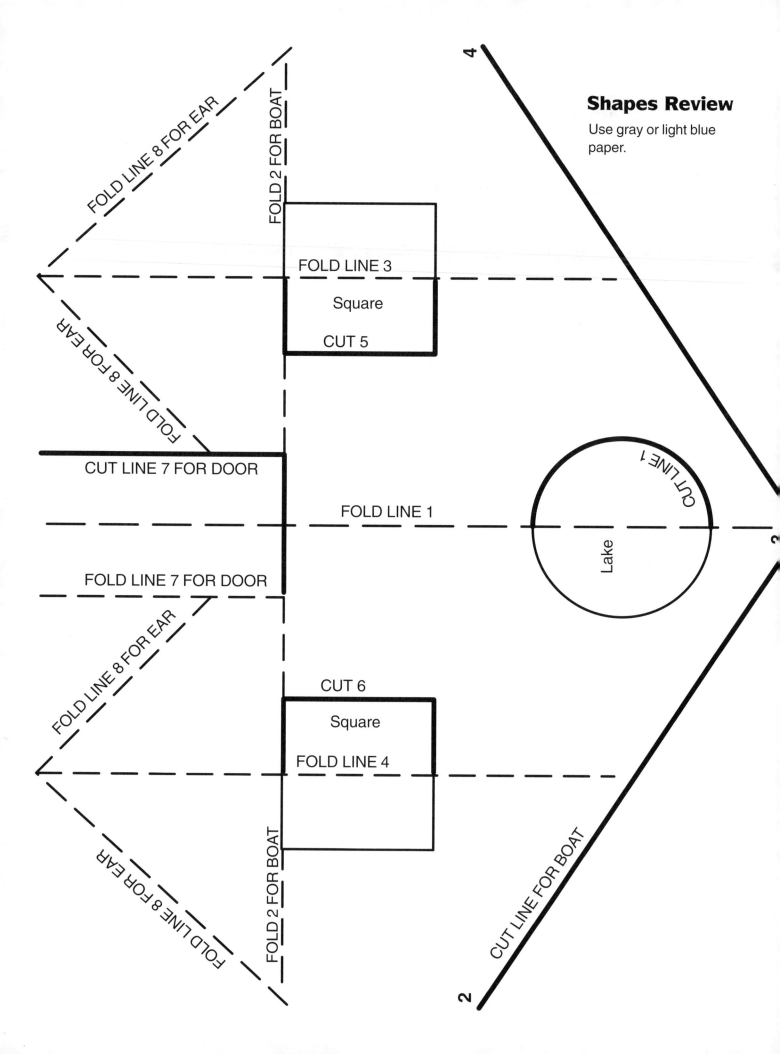

Shapes Review

Use gray or light blue paper.

FOLD LINE 8 FOR EAR

FOLD 2 FOR BOAT

4

FOLD LINE 3

Square

CUT 5

FOLD LINE 8 FOR EAR

CUT LINE 7 FOR DOOR

CUT LINE 1

FOLD LINE 1

Lake

FOLD LINE 7 FOR DOOR

FOLD LINE 8 FOR EAR

CUT 6

Square

FOLD LINE 4

FOLD LINE 8 FOR EAR

FOLD 2 FOR BOAT

CUT LINE FOR BOAT

2

One

It was a very hot summer day and Jason could barely stand the heat. In fact, he felt very much like the black plastic pocket comb that someone had dropped on the sidewalk. Jason kicked it absentmindedly with his foot. The comb was starting to melt from the heat, and Jason felt like he was, too. **(Cut 1 to 2.)**

Have you ever felt as hot as Jason? Jason walked down the street, looking for a way to cool off. **(Cut 3 to 4.)** What are some ways that you like to cool off in the summer? **(Accept suggestions from the children. As they name a way to cool off, repeat their suggestion and cut out the next tooth of the comb.)** For example—Yes, Jason could go swimming. So Jason walked to the swimming pool. **(Cut from 5 to 6. Set aside cutouts.)**

These are all very good ways to keep cool on a hot summer day. You could go swimming, run through the sprinkler, lay in the cool grass. **(Unfold at line 2 only and show comb upside down to represent blades of grass.)**

But Jason also wanted something to drink to help him stay cooler. He thought about this as he lay in the cool green grass. What do you like to drink when you are hot? Yes, those are all drinks to cool you off. Jason's favorite drink was orange juice, but he wanted to make it really, really cold. How do you think you could make orange juice really cold? Is there anything you could do to it? Yes, Jason decided to put his orange juice in the freezer to make it really cold. But when he reached in the freezer to get out his cup of orange juice, the orange juice was stuck in the cup. Why was that?

Jason could not get his frozen orange juice out of the cup. How do you think Jason might solve his problem? **(Accept answers from the children.)**

What do you think that Jason could do next time that he was hot and wanted some frozen orange juice? Yes, he could put a stick in his cup before he put it in the freezer. That way when the orange juice froze, the stick would freeze with it and Jason would have a handle to eat it with.

This food has a special name. Do you know what we call this food? Yes, it's a Popsicle. The handle of a Popsicle is usually a … yes, a Popsicle stick. You know this Popsicle stick actually reminds me of a special number. **(Unfold and hold up cut out for popsicle stick.)** Do you know what number that is? Yes, it is a number ONE.

Remember at the beginning of the story when Jason was so hot that he felt like the melting comb on the sidewalk? Look carefully at this comb. **(Hold comb up again. Paper should remain folded on fold line 1.)** Do you see any number ones in this comb? Yes, all the teeth are number ones.

The next time that you comb your hair, look carefully at your comb and notice how many number ones are standing in line just to comb your hair. When you eat your next Popsicle, look carefully at the stick. It is also going to remind you of the number one.

☄ Activities

1. Mix up juice, pour into paper cups, place Popsicle sticks in middle and freeze.

2. Let children make projects with Popsicle sticks and glue.

3. Ask children to draw a picture of themselves combing their hair, or going to a barber shop for a haircut.

4. Look for the number one in your classroom or library. Number ones can be found on keyboards, clocks, bulletin boards, telephones. Is there anything in the room that reminds you of the number one? What about a door, narrow window or end of a shelving unit?

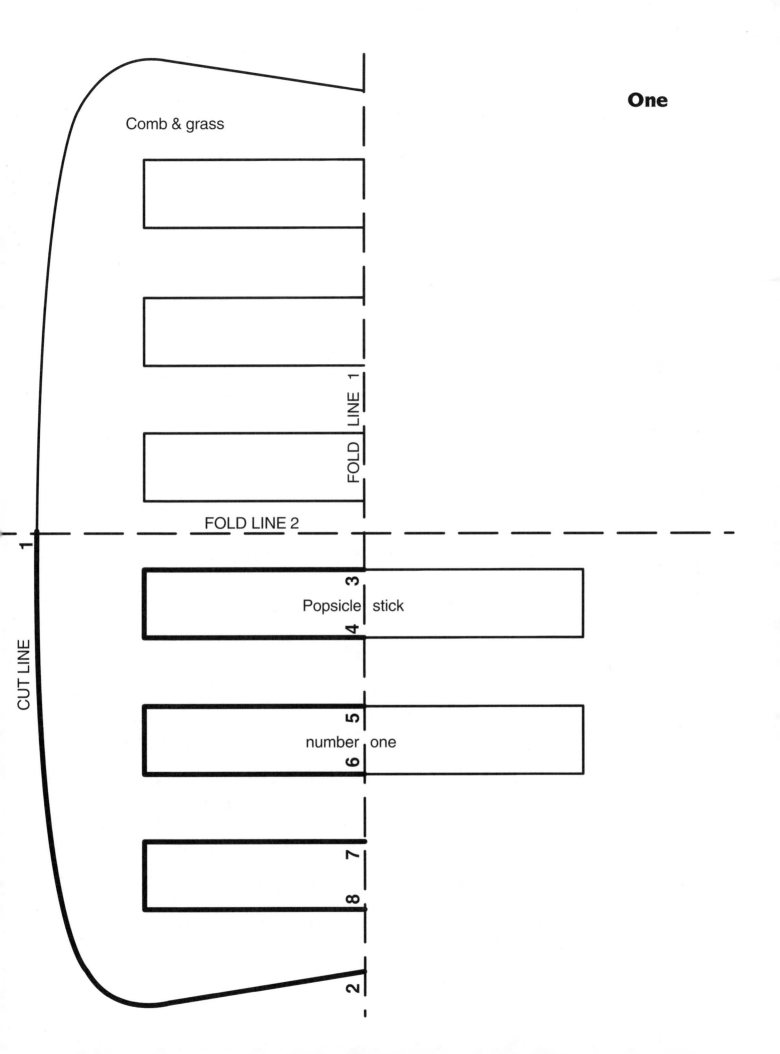

One

Comb & grass

FOLD LINE 1

FOLD LINE 2

CUT LINE

1

3

Popsicle stick

4

5

number one

6

7

8

2

Two

A Variation of the West African Folktale "The Bad Habit"

This is the story of two friends —Rabbit and Fish. They were friends because they liked to tell each other stories. It was a great way to entertain one another and pass the time.

One day Rabbit had gone down to the water's edge to visit with Fish. **(Cut from 1 to 2.)** She started telling Fish a story but Fish interrupted her, "Rabbit, it sounds like an interesting story that you are telling me, but I am finding that I really can't pay attention to it."

Rabbit said, "I thought you liked my stories. Why don't you want to listen?"

Fish answered, "Because Rabbit, you are hopping around, twitching your ears, wiggling your nose, sniffing the air, and waving your paws. It is so distracting that I can't concentrate on your story!" **(Cut from 2 to 3.)**

Rabbit replied, "I'm distracting? What about you? The entire time I am trying to talk, you are swimming back and forth and back and forth in front of me. **(Cut from 3 to 4.)** Come to think of it, I have never seen you not swimming! Can you float without swimming?"

"Of course I can!" Fish answered. "But I bet you can't stand perfectly still."

Rabbit answered, "Oh yes, I can! But I bet you can't float without swimming."

Fish said, "Well, let's just have a contest and see who wins. When I count to three, we will both be perfectly still. The first one who moves, loses. Agreed?" **(Cut from 4 to 5.)**

Rabbit said, "Agreed."

Fish said, "One, Two, Three, Start!"

Rabbit did not move. Fish did not swim.

After about two minutes, Rabbit felt awful. She had never had so many wiggles that needed wiggling.

After about two more minutes, Fish felt awful. He did not quite know how to float—he had never done it before. Fish even thought he might drown if he didn't keep swimming. **(Cut from 5 to 6.)**

Rabbit said, "Fish, while we are waiting for you to start swimming again and lose the contest, let me finish my story. Since I am being perfectly still, you will have no trouble paying attention to me. Let me see, where was I? Oh yes, I was telling you about our friend Squirrel. I was hopping by his tree—like this. **(Storyteller moves legs.)** I wrinkled up my nose to sniff the air because I smelled smoke—like this. **(Sniff air.)** I saw Squirrel waving at me—like this. I hopped right over to his tree—like this. **(Wave hand.)** Squirrel had tried to build a fire to roast acorns but it got too smokey. So I waved my ears and cleared the smoke —like this. I, Rabbit, solved Squirrel's problem." **(Cut 6 back to 1, and show Rabbit only.)**

Fish immediately caught on to Rabbit's trick. He said, "Good thing for Squirrel that you came along when you did, Rabbit. That reminds me of the time last summer when I had to help Mother Duck with her little ducklings. Did I ever tell you about it? A big thunderstorm blew in very quickly that afternoon and Mother Duck did not have time to gather all of her little ducklings close to her. The thunder was so loud that it scared the ducklings. They did not know what to do. They were swimming every which way—like this. **(Show swimming action.)** I swam over to Mother Duck—like this. I told her I would help her by swimming underneath the ducklings—like this. I guided them to safety." **(Separate papers and show Fish.)**

When Fish finished talking, Rabbit said, "Wow! What a story! Good thing we can entertain ourselves with stories. But I can't think of any other stories right now. Can we end our contest and just say that both of us won?"

Fish said, "Good idea. That was a really silly contest anyway."

And that's the story of the two friends—Rabbit and Fish.

⭐ Activities

1. Discuss why Rabbit and Fish each acted out the story that they told. What did this give them the chance to do?

2. Ask the children if they have ever had a "stare down" contest with a friend. Explain what a "stare down" contest is if necessary. If time permits, let everyone choose a partner and try it.

3. Photocopy pattern on the next page and let everyone cut it out. Children may add facial features with markers or crayons. Children may glue Popsicle sticks on to cutouts to make puppets. Retell the story together.

4. Discuss all of the 'twos' in the story—two friends, two faces, two ears which become two fins, two trick stories. Continue the discussion of 'two' by asking what comes in sets of two—shoes, socks, mittens, hands, eyes, ears, earrings, arms, legs, bicycle tires, boots, and so on.

Add these fish and rabbit facial features for story.

Two

Before cutting, add rabbit and fish facial features to back (hidden) sides of papers. Use two colors of paper if desired (i.e. pink for rabbit and light blue for fish.)

5

3

4

6

2

1 CUT LINE

Three

Does your name start with the letter C? Do you have a C in your first name? What about your last name? Do you have a C in it? Here is the letter C. **(Cut out letter C from folded paper.)** C is an important letter, isn't it? One of my favorite friend's name starts with the letter C. Her name is Celeste. **(If one of your listeners has a name that starts with a C, use his or her name.)**

When Celeste was a little girl, she loved to go out to eat. On Celeste's birthday, she was particularly excited. She knew that her mom was going to take her to any restaurant that she wanted. It was a family birthday tradition. All her brothers and sisters had gotten to choose one every year since they turned three. Now Celeste herself was finally old enough for this privilege!

Celeste's mom said to her, "Today is your birthday, big girl. And I get to take you out to eat for your birthday. Where would you like to go, sweetheart?"

Celeste said, "I want to go someplace that has swings, Mommy. I want to eat and then swing on the swings." **(Show upside down C for swing.)**

Then Celeste said, "I also want seats, Mommy. And I want a surprise toy in my lunch." **(Turn C over to show how it could be a stool.)**

"Yes, Celeste. But what kind of food do you want to eat?" asked her mom.

"Catsup," said Celeste, "I'd like catsup and some french fries and chicken nuggets." Does anyone know what letter the word catsup begins with? What letter does the word chicken begin with? Yes, catsup and chicken begin with the letter "C." **(Turn stool to show letter C again.)** Celeste's mother said, "I still do not know where you want to eat."

"Guess! I want swings, seats, catsup, and a toy!" said Celeste.

Which eating place do you think Celeste wanted to go to? Yes, those are all great places to eat, and Celeste could eat her birthday dinner at any of those restaurants.

Celeste said, " I want to eat dinner with my favorite person! It is my …" Do you know who her favorite person is? Yes, it is her mom! Did you notice that this cutout also makes a letter M? **(Unfold C and show M.)** M is for mother. How many of you already know that?

Celeste's mom gave her a big birthday hug and said, "Okay, let's go get Celeste some chicken nuggets, catsup, a toy and then swing on the swings." **(Fold into C for Celeste, and catsup.)**

I bet you noticed something special about our M for Mom. Does this remind you of a number? Yes, it is also the number 3. **(Turn M to show 3.)** That's because moms are favorite people for lots of three year olds!

Do you remember a long time ago when you were three? Raise your hand if it was a real treat to go out and eat with your mom then. Do you still like to go out to eat with your mom? Yes, I do too.

Activities

1. Provide cutouts of the number three and encourage children to glue or color sets of three on the number three.

2. Read stories involving the number three, "Three Bears," "Three Pigs," "Three Sillies," "Three Billy Goats," etc.

3. Provide cereal of different colors and sort them into sets of three. Then eat!

4. Color a picture of your three favorite foods, three favorite stories, activities, etc.

Three

Use any color of paper.

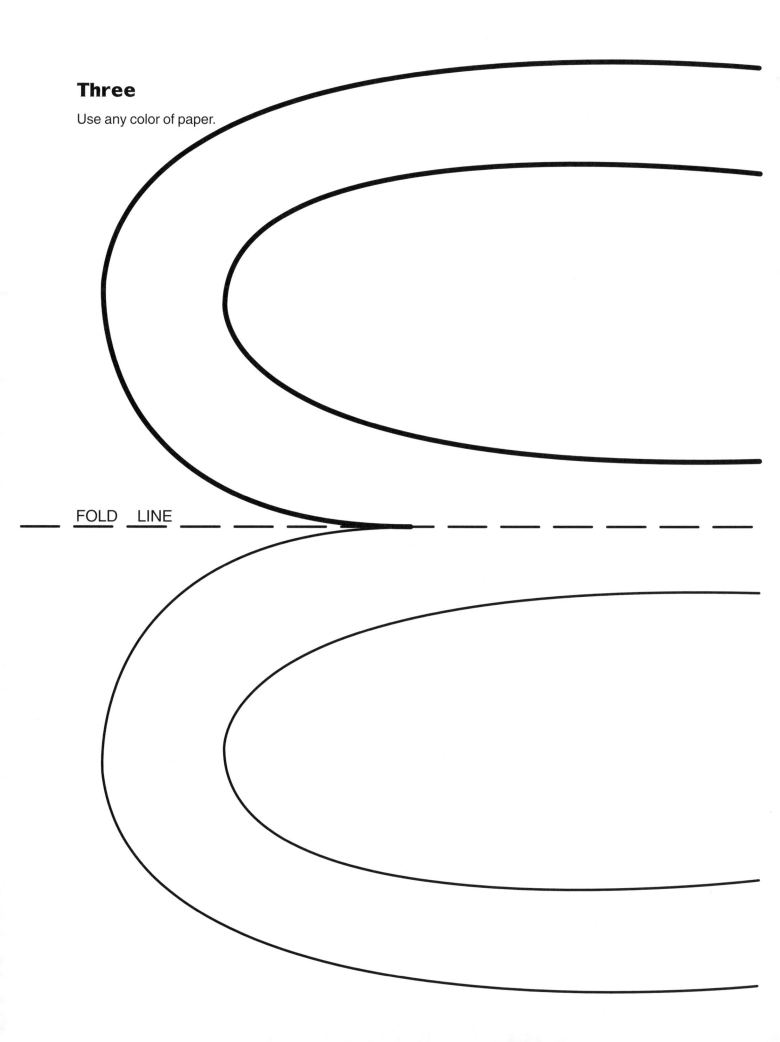

FOLD LINE

Four

Have you ever done a silly thing? A silly thing would be something you did that just did not make any sense, like putting away the box of ice cream in the cupboard instead of the freezer, or taking a bath with your socks on. **(If time permits, share something silly that you have done and/or ask listeners to share their "silly" stories.)**

In stories, sometimes people who do silly things are called "Sillies." So now you know what a Silly is. A Silly is a person who does not have very much sense. He or she has trouble figuring things out. Here is a silly story about four Sillies.

Far ago there were four Sillies. They were the best of friends and did everything together. They wanted to be alike in every way, so they lived in four houses in a row that were just alike. **(Cut from 1 to 2 and 3 to 4.)**

The Sillies visited each other all the time. The four doors to their houses were just alike too. **(Pull pieces of paper apart but keep folded, and show door openings.)** What shape are the doors? Yes, they are all rectangles.

One day the four Sillies went grocery shopping, and then they were going to eat lunch together. They decided to eat peanut butter and jelly sandwiches for lunch. What do you need in order to make a peanut butter and jelly sandwich? Yes, you need bread, peanut butter, and jelly. But one Silly did not like jelly. So he bought bananas instead. Have you ever eaten bananas on your peanut butter sandwich instead of jelly?

The four Sillies decided to eat lunch at the house of the first Silly. The first Silly said, "You must each bring your own chair because I only have one chair."

The Sillies walked over to the first Silly's house. **(Unfold and cut from 5 to 6 and 7 to 8.)**

They all carried their chairs. **(Cut papers in half from 9 to 10 and show four chairs.)** Here are their chairs. The second Silly put the loaf of bread on his chair as he carried it. The third Silly put the jelly on his chair as he carried it and the fourth Silly put the peanut butter on his chair as he carried it.

They arrived at the first Silly's house and asked, "Where is your table?"

The first Silly answered, "Oh, I don't have one."

The other Sillies asked, "Then where will we put the bread, jelly, bananas, and peanut butter to make our sandwiches?"

What do you think they should do for a table? Is there anything else they could use for a table? Yes, they could put all their chairs together and use them for a table. Have you ever sat on the floor and used a chair for a table? It's fun, isn't it?

So the four Sillies put the chairs together and made a table. They sat on the floor, fixed their sandwiches and then ate them. That worked out great.

But when the four Sillies were done eating and ready to go home, they could not find their chairs! They said, "Where are the chairs we brought?"

You know where the chairs are, don't you? What should the four Sillies do now? Yes, you are right. They should separate the table they made back into four chairs.

One Silly said, "I don't know about this table, but I am taking my chair and going home."

So each Silly took his own chair. And what do you think happened to the table? It disappeared!

Do you remember how many Sillies we had in our story? Yes, there were four Sillies. Here is our number four. **(Turn a chair over and show the number four.)**

Activities

1. Let each member of the class use their chair as a table for a particular activity.

2. As a group, discuss and look for the number four in the shape of chairs in your room. Which chairs make a four? Which ones do not? Are there any other pieces of furniture that have a number four hidden in them?

3. Retell the story and let each child cut out his or her own number four. (Depending on the age of your listeners, you may want to pre-trace a large number four on colored paper for each child.) Have the child color or glue four items (buttons, cereal pieces, etc.) on the four.

4. Let the children draw pictures of themselves doing something silly.

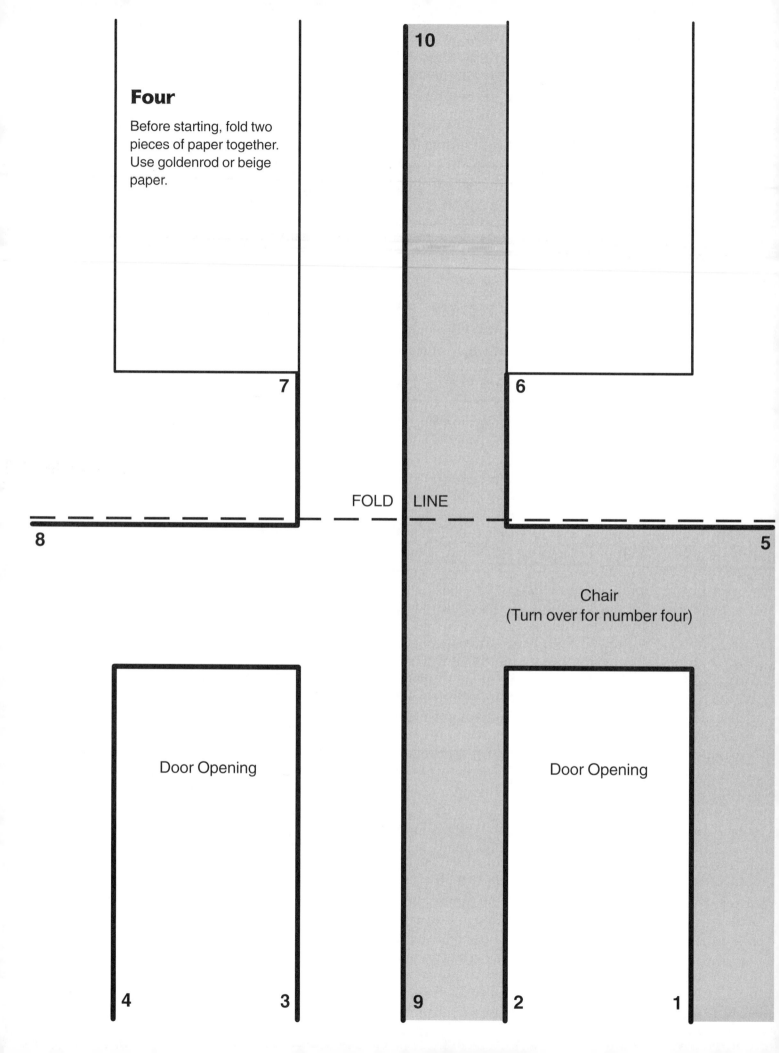

Four

Before starting, fold two pieces of paper together. Use goldenrod or beige paper.

10

7   **6**

FOLD LINE

8   **5**

Chair
(Turn over for number four)

Door Opening   Door Opening

4   **3**   **9**   **2**   **1**

Five

A trickster is an animal who is always trying to get something for nothing. You probably already know that Rabbit is a trickster. In this story all of Rabbit's friends are mad at him. Here's the story. **(Begin cutting out the number five and continue cutting as you tell the story.)**

On Monday, Rabbit tricked Turtle. Turtle was gathering acorns. Rabbit walked by carrying a cup. He said, "Turtle, You had better be careful walking around under that oak tree. What if one of those acorns fell off the tree and landed on your back? Your shell is so weak that it would probably crack if a nut landed on it. Here, let me help you test it. Just put some of your acorns in my cup and I will throw them at your shell. If it hurts, then you will know not to stand under an oak tree. Don't worry, I won't throw them too hard."

Turtle dropped five acorns into Rabbit's cup. Do you think Rabbit tested Turtle's shell? No, he hopped away as fast as he could.

On Tuesday, Rabbit tricked Elephant. Elephant was picking bananas from the highest part of the tree. Rabbit hopped by carrying a basket. He said, "Elephant, that trunk of yours is really long. But it seems so clumsy. It looks like you really can't do much with it. I bet you can't pick one of those bananas and drop it into this basket. Here, I will hold the basket up very close to you, and you see if you can drop the banana into it."

Elephant dropped a banana into Rabbit's basket. Rabbit said, "That was just a lucky shot. See if you can do it again." How many bananas do you think Rabbit tricked Elephant into dropping in his basket before Elephant realized that it was a trick? Yes, Rabbit got Elephant to give him five bananas.

On Wednesday, Rabbit tricked Coyote. Coyote was in his garden digging potatoes out of the ground. Rabbit walked by carrying a big bag. He called to Coyote, "Coyote, you are as ugly as those potatoes! Nobody should have to look at your potato head. See this bag? I brought it so that you can wear it over your head. You would look much better that way." When Coyote heard Rabbit say all those terrible things, he became so angry that he started throwing potatoes at Rabbit.

What do you think Rabbit did? Yes, he gathered up the potatoes in his bag and went home to make a nice big pot of potato soup. How many potatoes do you think Coyote threw at Rabbit? Yes, he threw five big potatoes at him.

On Thursday, Rabbit tricked Snake. Snake was sitting on top of a bird's nest. Rabbit hopped by. He was holding a frying pan. He called up to Snake, "I see that you have found some eggs. Just drop them down into this pan. I will make scrambled eggs for you. Have you ever had scrambled eggs? They are

55

delicious." With the tip of his nose, Snake pushed the eggs out of the nest and into Rabbit's frying pan. Do you think that Rabbit made scrambled eggs for Snake? No, as soon as five eggs landed in Rabbit's pan, he hopped off down the road. Snake was very angry with Rabbit.

On Friday, Rabbit tricked Crocodile. Crocodile was in the river. Rabbit hopped by carrying a bucket. He said, "Crocodile, you are great at catching fish. But I bet you are terrible at counting them. I bet you could not flip five fish out of the water with your tail, and count them at the same time. That would take too many brains. You have a big tail but a very little brain. I bet you are not smart enough to even try it."

Of course, that made Crocodile so mad that he immediately flipped five fish out of the water, counting them as he did it. What do you think Rabbit did? Yes, he quickly tossed the five fish in his bucket, and hopped away as fast as he could. **(Finish cutting out the number five and show to listeners.)**

During the time that Rabbit was playing all of these tricks on his friends, the rainy season in the jungle was starting. During this season, thunderstorms blow in and thoroughly drench everything.

Let's make a thunderstorm together right now.

> The thunderstorms start very slowly with a gentle breeze, like this. **(Rub your palms together back and forth.)** Can you do this with me?

> Then, a few raindrops fall, like this. **(Slowly snap your fingers.)** Can you do this with me? Then more and more raindrops fall. **(Snap fingers faster.)**

> Then, lots of big raindrops come down. **(Make clicking sound with your tongue.)** Can you do this with me?

> Finally, there are lots of raindrops and lots of thunderclaps. **(Slap your legs with your hands.)** Can you do this with me?

> Then, just as suddenly as thunderstorms start, they go away. There are big raindrops. **(Click tongue.)** There are small raindrops. **(Snap fingers.)** Finally, there is just a gentle breeze. **(Rub hands together.)** Then the sun comes back out and the storm is over.

Usually, all the animals stayed inside during the rainy season but they were all so mad at Rabbit that they decided to teach him a lesson. They would play their own tricks on him, rain or shine.

On Monday, Turtle decided to catch Rabbit. Turtle gathered up lots of acorns and put them in a big pile. Then he poured sticky honey all over them. He knew that Rabbit would come along and help himself to the acorns. And that is just what Rabbit did. He reached out to take five of the acorns and his little paws got stuck in the honey. So Rabbit put his feet on the acorn pile, and they got stuck in the honey too. Rabbit was really stuck. He could not escape. Turtle crawled up to Rabbit, shouting, "I caught you, Rabbit. I've got you now!" Just then it began to rain. At first there was just a little breeze … then small raindrops fell … finally there was thunder. **(Invite the children to do the motions with you.)** Just as suddenly as it came up, the thunderstorm went away. **(Do motions in reverse order.)**

What do you think happened to Rabbit and the honey with all of that rain? Yes, the rain washed the honey away and Rabbit escaped. Turtle was madder than ever!

On Tuesday, Elephant decided to catch Rabbit. He used his long tusks to dig a big pit in the middle of the jungle path. Then he threw five bananas down into the pit and waited for Rabbit to come along. He did not have to wait long. Rabbit hopped down the trail, saw the big pit with the bananas in the bottom of it and jumped right in. He did not even think about how he was going to get out. Elephant lumbered up to the edge of the hole and shouted down to Rabbit, "I caught you, Rabbit. I've got you now."

Just then it started to rain. **(Do motions.)** At first there was just a little breeze … then small raindrops fell … finally there was thunder. **(Invite the children to do the motions with you.)** Just as suddenly as it came up, the thunderstorm went away. **(Do motions in reverse order.)**

What do you think happened to Rabbit down in the pit in the rainstorm? Yes, the pit filled up with water and Rabbit floated to the top and climbed out. Elephant was madder than ever!

On Wednesday, Coyote decided to catch Rabbit. He put five potatoes down on the path and hid behind a bush. Soon Rabbit hopped by and stopped to pick up the potatoes. That is when Coyote picked up Rabbit with his sharp teeth and carried him far away. Coyote put Rabbit down next to a dry creek bed. Coyote had carried Rabbit so far away that Rabbit would never be able to find his way back home. Coyote ran away, shouting, "I've got you back now, Rabbit. We will never see you again."

Just then it started to rain. **(Do motions.)** At first there was just a little breeze … then small raindrops fell … finally there was thunder. **(Invite the children to do the motions with you.)** Just as suddenly as it came up, the thunderstorm went away. **(Do motions in reverse order.)**

What do you think happened to Rabbit out in the rainstorm? Rabbit remembered that he lived downstream and so he watched which way the water ran in the creek bed and he followed it. In no time at all, Rabbit was home. Coyote was madder than ever!

On Thursday, Snake decided to catch Rabbit. He built a cardboard box and put five eggs in it. He put the box in the middle of the jungle path. He did not have to wait long for Rabbit to come along, see the box, and hop into it to get the eggs. Snake jumped out from his hiding place, slammed the lid down and shouted, "I caught you, Rabbit. I've got you now."

Just then it started to rain. **(Do motions.)** At first there was just a little breeze ... then small raindrops fell ... finally there was thunder. **(Invite the children to do the motions with you.)** Just as suddenly as it came up, the thunderstorm went away. **(Do motions in reverse order.)**

Do you know what happens to cardboard when it rains? Yes, it gets soft and falls apart. The cardboard got so wet so fast that Rabbit was able to push his way out of the box before Snake even realized what was happening. Snake was madder than ever!

On Friday, Crocodile decided to catch Rabbit. He made a big pile of soil next to the riverbank. He put five fish next to the pile and hid behind it. Pretty soon, Rabbit came hopping down to the river bank to get a drink of water. He saw the five fish and bent down to pick them up. Just then, Crocodile used his strong tail to flip the pile of soil on top of Rabbit, completely burying him. He shouted, "I caught you, Rabbit. I've got you now."

Just then it started to rain. **(Do motions.)** At first there was just a little breeze ... then small raindrops fell ... finally there was thunder. **(Invite the children to do the motions with you.)** Just as suddenly as it came up, the thunderstorm went away. **(Do motions in reverse order.)**

Do you know what happens to loose soil in a heavy rainstorm? Yes, all of the soil covering Rabbit washed away. Rabbit wiped the mud off his paws, laughed at Crocodile and hopped away. Crocodile was madder than ever!

Thanks to the rainstorms, Rabbit was very lucky and escaped five times. All of his old friends were so angry with him, that to this very day they never speak to Rabbit.

✨ Activities

1. Discuss the groups of five in this story. There are five friends, five acorns, five potatoes, five eggs, five bananas, five fish, five tricks, and five days.

2. Encourage the children to draw a picture of their favorite animal from the story showing the way that this animal tried to trick Rabbit.

3. Photocopy the number five and let each child cut it out and color it.

4. Discuss other animals that could be added to this story. What food could Rabbit trick them out of and what trap would they build to catch him?

Five

Use green
paper.

Six

Think way back to when you were a little tiny baby. What could you do? Could you walk? Could you talk? Could you say your name? No, you could not do any of these things. Now, you can do all of these things and more.

As you grow older, you learn to do more and more things. Now, I am thinking of a magic number of how old children usually are when they learn to do lots of important, independent things. See if you can guess what this number is. I will give you some hints.

When you are this age, your mother usually lets you walk a short way down the street to your friend's house. **(Cut from 1 to 2.)**

When you are this age, you can call your friends on the telephone to make plans or ask them something about school. **(Cut from 3 to 4. Hold telephone receiver to your ear.)**

Look at this. **(Open out and hold up piece that you just cut out.)** You are now big enough to eat an entire apple, right down to the core.

And when you are this particular age, you are old enough to eat your lunch at school. If you want to buy a lunch, you bring your lunch money to school. **(Cut from 5 to 6 and 7 to 8. Open out half circles to represent coins.)**

And, by the time you reach this special age, you have learned how important and fun it is to share with your friends. You can share toys, books, jokes, and even friends.

Does anyone know how old you have to be to do all of these things? What magic number am I thinking of? Yes, that is right. The number that I am thinking of is SIX. Is there anyone here today who is six years old?

This could be a pair of glasses or binoculars. **(Open out and show your paper cutout.)** When you are six years old, you are old enough to know how to use a pair of binoculars.

But this is not a six, is it? Wait a minute, remember that we said it is important that we share with our friends? By the time you are six years old you are really good at sharing, aren't you?

Maybe I can share my cutout with my friend here. **(Indicate one of the children.)** Let's see how I might do that. **(Cut sixes apart on lines indicated, 9 to 10 and 11 to 12. Show both sixes. Give one to a six-year-old listener.)**

Do you know what number this is? What if we put these two numbers side by side? Do you know what number two sixes next to each other make? Yes, that is correct. They make the number sixty-six.

Six is a very important number, isn't it? Does anyone have any other ideas about what you can do when you are six?

Six

✨ Activities

1. If you have access to a die-cutting machine, cut several number sixes for each child. Let children string them on a wrapping paper ribbon to make a "six" necklace.

2. Have an autograph party. Give each child a piece of paper. Encourage them to collect autographs from six friends.

3. Sing some songs that have the number six in them. "Sing a Song of Sixpence" is a six song. It is fun to make number changes to well-known songs. Change "Three Bind Mice" to "Six Blind Mice." Change "Five Little Ducks" to "Six Little Ducks."

4. Make a bar graph to represent who has dogs for pets and who has cats for pets. Let each child color in a box for their dog and/or cat. If children have other types of pets, include them in your bar graph. Are there more than six of any one type of pet? Which type of pet does the class have the most of?

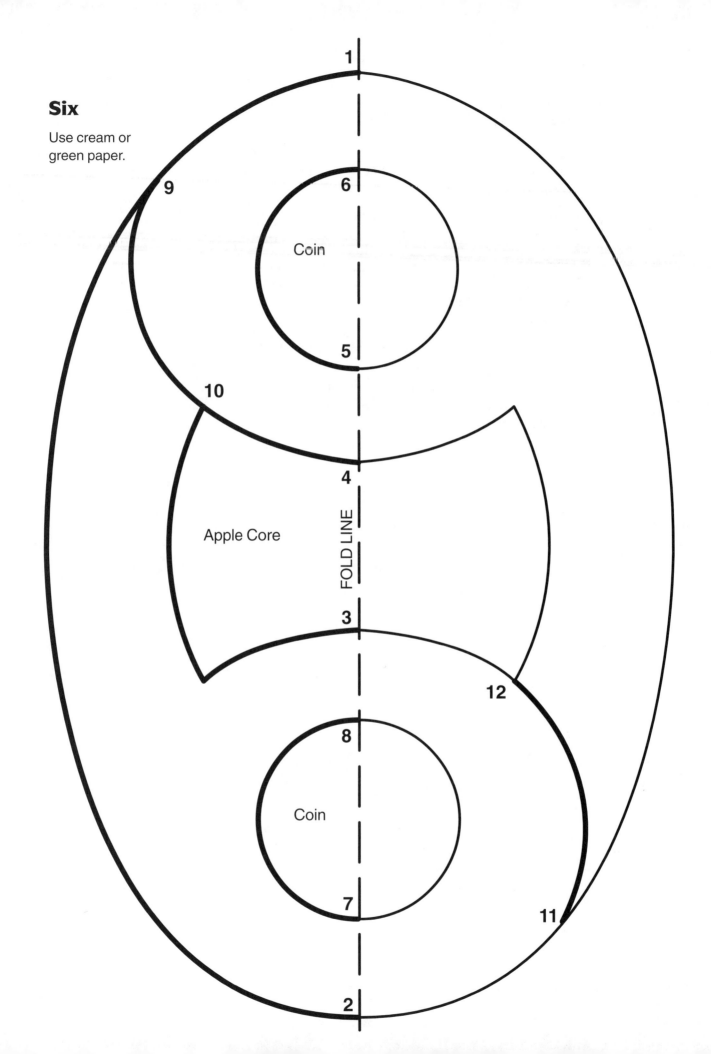

Six

Use cream or
green paper.

1

9

6

Coin

5

10

4

Apple Core

FOLD LINE

3

12

8

Coin

7

11

2

Seven
Variation of a Japanese Folktale

Imagine a boat full of monkeys, because that is how this story begins—with a boat full of monkeys. These monkeys were going to an island in the middle of the lake to have a picnic. They did not bring their food with them because there was already food on the island. What do monkeys like to eat? Yes, they like to eat bananas. I bet you know where bananas grow. That is right—on trees.

As soon as they arrived at the island, the monkeys saw millions of bananas. They were sooo hungry. They all jumped out of the boat and started climbing the trees to get bananas. **(Cut from 1 to 2.)**

Not one monkey thought about the boat—so not one monkey tied up the boat. What do you think happened? Yes, the boat floated away.

When it started to get dark, the monkeys began to think about going home. But they could not find their boat. After hours of searching, the monkeys decided that the next morning was soon enough to figure out how to get home. They were very tired and settled down to sleep in the trees. **(Cut from 2 to 3.)**

The next morning, one of the little monkeys had a big surprise, for there was a crocodile waiting for him just as he got to the bottom of his tree. The crocodile said, "Good morning, Little Monkey. Thank you for showing up to be my breakfast today."

Little Monkey said, "Oh, but I cannot be your breakfast today. Actually, I was just leaving your island. Now, if you will excuse me, please." **(Cut inside, 4.)**

The crocodile answered, "Little Monkey, you are not leaving. Your boat floated away yesterday, so you and your little friends are stuck here on my island. Every morning, I am going to eat one of you tasty little monkeys for breakfast and you get to be first."

Little Monkey replied, "Very well, if you insist. But just let me say good-bye to my friends before you eat me."

The crocodile yawned and said, "Fair enough. I will give you seven minutes to say good-bye to your friends before I eat you. Quickly now before my seven minute timer runs out." **(Open up cutout and show timer.)**

Soon Little Monkey came back with all of his friends. He said, "Look at all my friends, Mr. Crocodile. I bet that you don't have as many friends as I do. Watch me count my friends."

Let's help Little Monkey count his friends. One … Two … Three … Four … Five … Six … Seven.**(Hold up seven fingers.)**

Then Little Monkey said, "I bet you don't have as many friends as I do, Mr. Crocodile. Why, I bet that you don't have <u>any</u> friends!"

Mr. Crocodile said, "Oh, yes I do! I have just as many friends as you! I bet that I even have more than you! Wait right there while I go and get them."

Mr. Crocodile splashed into the water and started calling for all of his friends to come. They swam in from all directions with splashes and growls.

Mr. Crocodile then turned to Little Monkey and said, "There! What did I tell you! Look how many friends I have. I have many more friends than you, Little Monkey."

Little Monkey said, "More than seven? I don't think you have seven friends in the water with you. They are all swimming and thrashing around so much that all I see are a few backs, tails, and snouts. You probably really only have three or four friends out there."

Mr. Crocodile said, "Well, I can prove to you that there are certainly more than seven crocodile friends out here in the water. Here, we will line up and then you can count us."

Mr. Crocodile had all of his friends line up in a row. There were so many crocodiles that they stretched from the island all the way across the lake to the shore. Then he called to Little Monkey, "Now, count us!"

Little Monkey said to Mr. Crocodile, "Okay, now that is more like it! To make sure that I don't lose count, I will hop on each one of your friends as I count them. Turn your timer over and see if I can do this in seven minutes. And tell your friends to keep their mouths shut, will you?" **(Turn timer over.)**

Little Monkey called to his seven monkey friends, "Come here and help me count all of Mr. Crocodile's friends. He thinks that he has more than seven. Let's count them."

Little Monkey and his friends hopped from one crocodile's back to the next. Little Monkey, who was at the end of the line, counted as they all went across. "One … Two … Three … Four … Five … Six … Seven … Eight … Nine …" As Little Monkey hopped off the last crocodile's back and shouted "Ten," they were all safely back on land! **(Cut the timer at the fold line and at point 2.)**

Little Monkey said, "Mr. Crocodile, it looks like you were right. You do have more than seven friends. And thank you for helping us get back home."

With that, Little Monkey and his friends scampered away, leaving behind the hungry crocodiles and the number seven.

Here is Little Monkey's number seven, for the seven monkey friends that helped him trick Mr. Crocodile. **(Hold up number seven cutouts.)**

Seven

✦ Activities

1. Let the children string seven monkeys together from a "Barrel of Monkeys" game.

2. Show and discuss a sand timer from a game. Explain how it works. Then see how many jumping jacks, toe touches, etc., that the class can do before the timer runs out.

3. Sing "Five Little Monkeys Jumping On a Bed" but change the five to a seven. Other songs that are easy to adapt to seven are "Five Little Ducks" and "Five Little Monkeys Swinging in a Tree, Teasing Mr. Crocodile."

4. Practice writing the number seven using the familiar rhyme of "Across the sky and down from heaven, That's the way we make a seven."

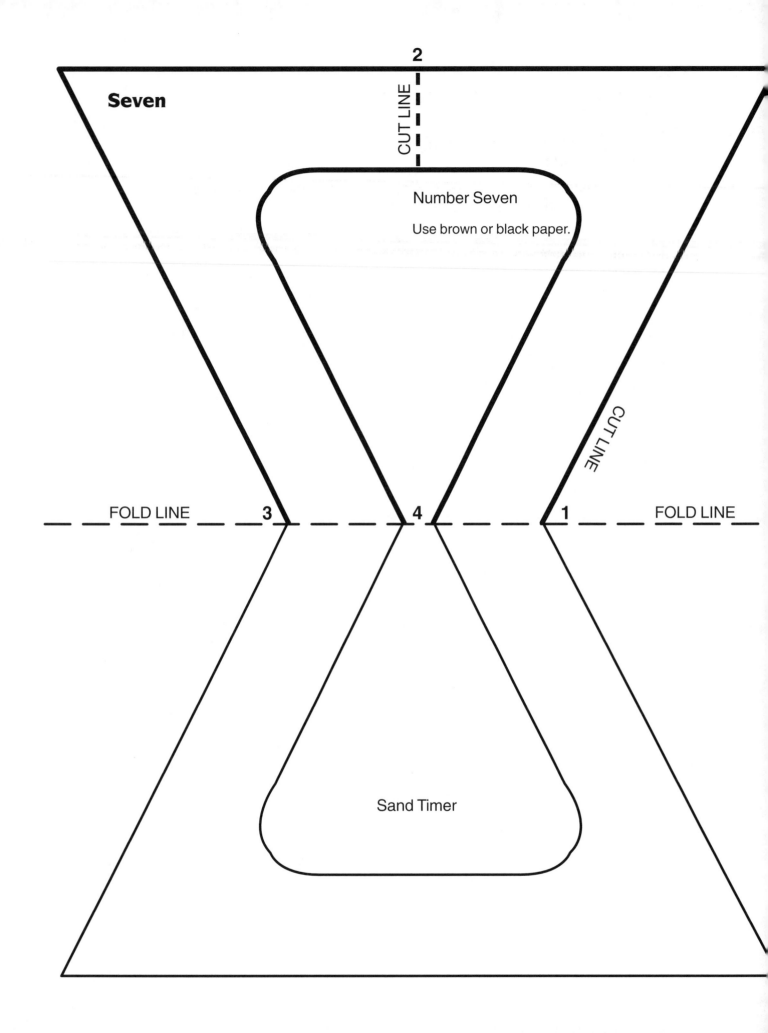

Eight

Have you ever seen a horse run, or watched a horse race? Once there was a very fast horse. He could run like the wind. But because this horse rarely ran just for fun, people thought that he did not like to run. The horse only ran when the owner forced him. So everyone called the horse—Walker.

Everyday after school, Weston would get off the bus right in front of Walker's field. Weston always saved an apple or some carrot sticks from his lunch to feed to Walker. When Walker saw Weston, sometimes he would run up to the fence, but most of the time he would just walk to greet Weston and receive his snack. Weston spent time visiting with his friend Walker before going down the lane to his family's farm.

One day, Walker's owner was there when Weston got off the bus. He told Weston that he was going to sell Walker soon.

"Why?" asked Weston. "Walker is a perfectly good horse. He is a fast runner too."

The owner answered, "I know, Weston. But Walker does not like to run. You can tell that Walker does not enjoy running. Have you noticed that about him?"

Weston replied, "I've noticed that Walker doesn't run often, but when he does run, he can run as fast as the wind."

The owner said, "Well, Weston, I just wanted you to know that I am planning on selling Walker in a few weeks, so that you will not be surprised when he is gone."

The next afternoon it was raining as Weston got off the bus and went over to the fence. He whistled for Walker, who came over very slowly. Weston noticed that when Walker walked across the field, the mud made a sucking noise as the horse pulled his feet out of it. **(Cut from 1 to 2.)**

After that day, it did not rain again for a long time. The ground became very dry and Weston noticed that Walker did more running. That gave Weston an idea.

The next day he saw Walker's owner and said, "I noticed that when the ground is dry, Walker likes to run in his field. But if the ground is the least bit damp or muddy, Walker only walks. Around here we rarely have perfectly dry ground. Maybe the condition of the ground has something to do with Walker running. Perhaps if you changed his horseshoes, Walker would do more running." **(Cut from 3 to 4, and show horseshoe.)**

"What a great idea, Weston. I will take your suggestion," said Walker's owner.

Walker's horseshoes were changed to make him more comfortable, and Walker was so happy that he spent hours running around the pasture.

Walker ran so well that his owner decided to enter him in a local horse race. The day before the race, Weston said to Walker's owner, "I made Walker something in school today. Put this on his saddle so he will have good luck in the race tomorrow."

The owner unfolded the piece of paper. Weston said, "That is my lucky number, so maybe it will be lucky for Walker too."

Do you know what the lucky number was? Yes, it was a number eight! **(Unfold the horseshoes to show the number eight.)**

Number eight was very lucky for Walker because he won the race the next day. Walker went on to win many races after that. In fact, as a race horse, Walker's owner changed his name to Number Eight. And because of Weston's suggestion to change his horseshoes, Number Eight became one of the greatest race horses of all time. **(Show number eight again.)**

Activities

1. Ask the listeners what their favorite or lucky number is and why.

2. Discuss other things that the number eight resembles such as a race track, snowman, or eyeglasses.

3. Teach the children how to play the card game "Crazy Eights."

4. Let everyone have a chance to write the number eight using finger paint, a sand tray, crayons, markers, or pencils. Teach them the well-known rhyme, "We make an S but do not wait, we climb back up to make an eight."

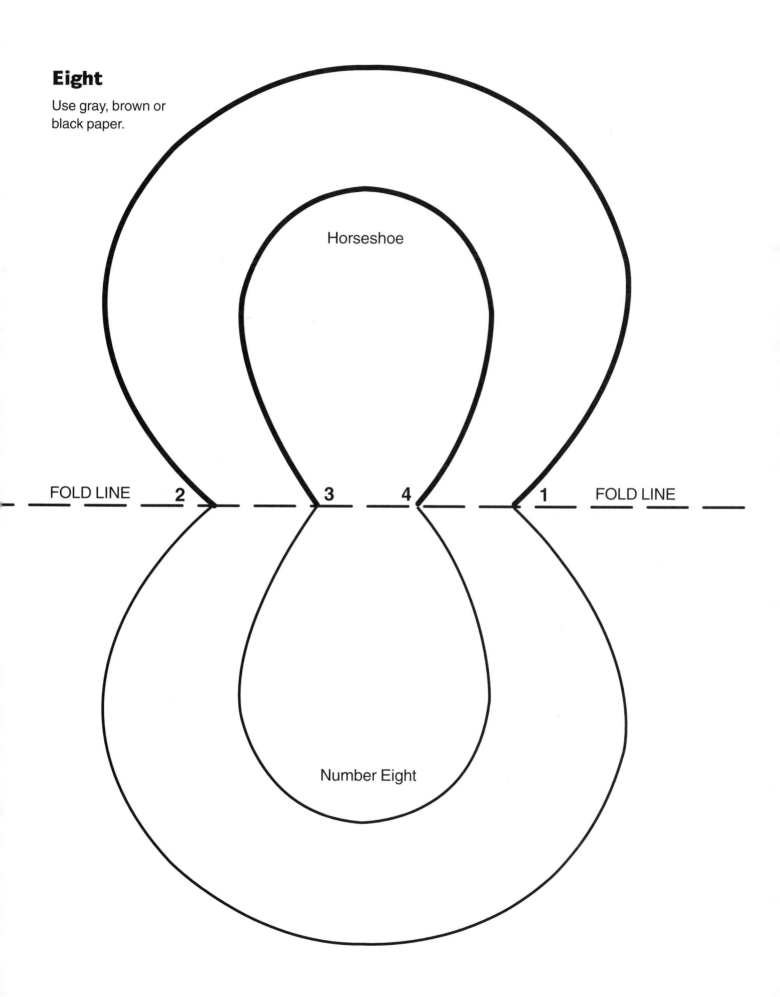

Eight

Use gray, brown or black paper.

Horseshoe

FOLD LINE   **2**   **3**   **4**   **1**   FOLD LINE

Number Eight

Nine

One day, Crow flew down and landed on a low tree branch. As soon as he had landed, Crow noticed a snail crawling slowly by. Crow had not eaten in many days and was very hungry. He was so hungry in fact, that even this large, slimy snail looked good enough to eat.

But do you know what snails always carry around with them on their backs? Yes, they carry their houses around with them. These snail houses are called shells.

Crow knew that he would have to get Snail to crawl out of his shell before he could eat him. But how? Snail hardly ever crawled all the way out of his house, so Crow would somehow have to trick Snail into leaving his shell.

Crow leaned over from his perch on the branch and called down to Snail, "Hello there, Snail. How are you? I say, you look rather small today. I mean your shell is the same size, but you, yourself, look a lot smaller. I saw you just last week and I thought you were a lot bigger. Did you shrink or something?" **(Cut from 1 to 2 to 3 to 4, snail's shell.)** Here is snail's shell.

Snail lifted his head and looked at crow sitting on the branch. He answered, "Crow, I have been the same size for a long time now. You are just imagining things."

Crow said, "No, I am serious, Snail. You really do seem smaller. Are you sure that you are okay? I am really worried about you."

Snail answered, "Crow, I tell you that I am the same size I've always been. But thank you for your concern." And Snail started sliding away slowly.

Crow said, "Wait, Snail! Could you just show me that you are okay? Just crawl out of your shell a bit so that I will know that you are the same size."

Snail started to scoot out of his shell. As soon as Snail was about halfway out of his shell, Crow flew down from his branch and grabbed Snail's shell with his beak. He shook it back and forth until Snail fell the rest of the way out.

Snail was very angry and yelled, "Crow, give me back my shell. You tricked me, didn't you?!"

Crow set Snail's shell on the ground behind him and chuckled, "Yes, indeed. And now Snail, I am going to eat you."

Snail said, "Wait, Crow. I must admit, that was a very good trick. But one good trick deserves another. Let me do a trick with you before you eat me. Oh, I know that you are too smart to fall for any of my silliness, but just let me try anyway. It is only fair."

Nine

Crow said, "No way, I am too hungry to wait while you think up some silly way to trick me. Besides, no one has never ever been able to trick me, and you can't either."

Snail said, "Fine, Crow. I agree with that. How about one short question instead? If you answer my question correctly, you get to eat me. But if you get it wrong, I get to have my shell back, okay?"

Crow nodded his head in agreement. **(Cut from 5 to 6.)** Snail said, "Here is the question. What is my favorite number? You get three guesses."

Crow said, "That is an easy question, and I'm a good guesser. Is this your favorite number?… Number seven?" **(Hold paper so listeners see the number seven. Make sure seven is facing the correct way.)**

Snail answered, "No, my favorite number is not seven. You get two more guesses." **(Fold snail shell in half. Cut circle out, point 7.)**

Crow guessed, "Is this your favorite number?…Number zero?" **(Hold paper so that listeners can see the zero.)**

Snail said, "No, it is not a zero. Last guess and then I get my shell back."

Crow said, "Well, how about one? Is your favorite number one?" **(Cut from 6 to 8, and show number one.)**

Snail said, "No, it is not one. Now please give me back my shell."

Crow said, "I will not give you back your shell until you tell me your favorite number."

Snail said, "I will not tell you my favorite number, I will show you!" **(Fold back seven, snail's head, and hold paper so audience can see the nine.)**

Do you know what Snail's favorite number is? Yes, it is the number nine!

Crow was so mad at Snail that he threw Snail's shell back to him and said, "There's your silly shell back. I did not want to eat you anyway, you slimy old thing!"

Snail crawled back in his shell and Crow flew away.

And to this day, Crows never even try to eat Snails! **(Open out paper and show snail again.)**

✨ Activities

1. Discuss the sequence of the story. What happened first, second, third, last?

2. Encourage the children to name some words that rhyme with the number nine, such as dine, line, fine, mine, pine, vine, shine.

3. As a group, do some exercises nine times. Count as you do nine jumping jacks, touch toes nine times, hop in place nine times, and jump up and down nine times.

4. Let every child work with a partner to form the shape of a number nine with their bodies. One person could scrunch themselves up into a ball and the other partner could stretch themselves out to make the line.

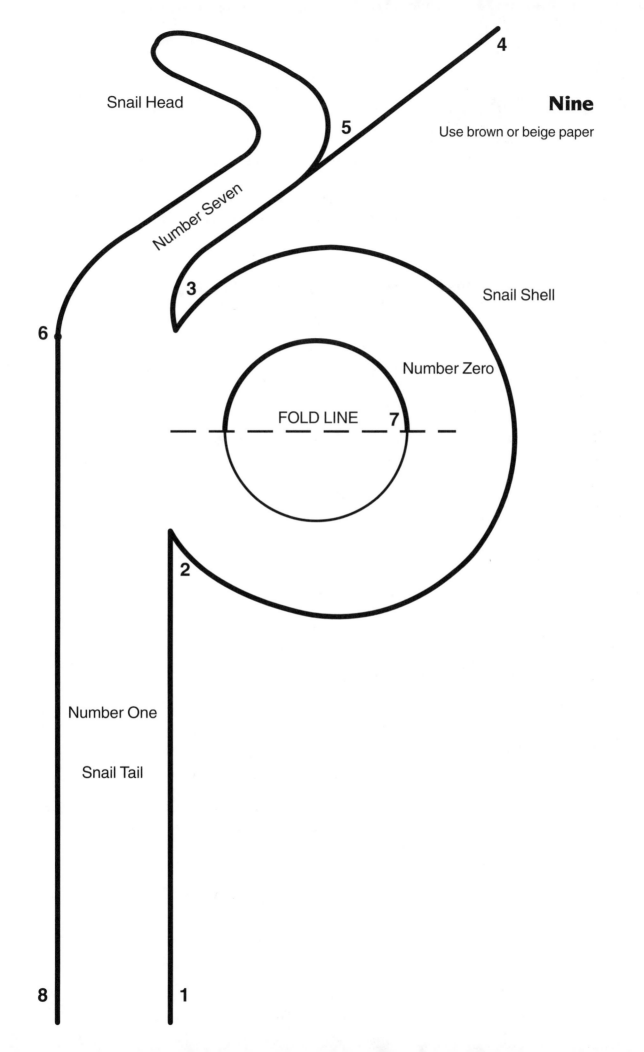

Snail Head

Number Seven

5

4

Nine

Use brown or beige paper

3

Snail Shell

6

Number Zero

FOLD LINE 7

2

Number One

Snail Tail

8 1

Ten

Variation of a Native American Folktale

For a long time, Mr. Sun, Mr. Rain, and Mr. Wind had been good friends. They worked together for many years to bring us all kinds of weather. But one day, Mr. Sun, Mr. Rain, and Mr. Wind had a discussion about who was the strongest of the three.

Mr. Wind said, "I'm so strong. I can hold a kite up in the air for hours. I can blow your garbage cans down the street, and sailboats across the lake. Here is a chant about me." Then Mr. Wind said, "Mr. Wind, I'm the man. If I can't do it, nobody can."

Let's say Mr. Wind's chant together.

> Mr. Wind, I'm the man.
> If I can't do it, nobody can.

But Mr. Rain said, "Wait a minute. I am also strong. I can fill the lakes that make the sailboats float. I can make people stay in their homes and not go on picnics. Listen to this chant about me." Then Mr. Rain said, "Mr. Rain, I'm the man. If I can't do it, nobody can."

Let's say Mr. Rain's chant together.

> Mr. Rain, I'm the man.
> If I can't do it, nobody can.

Finally Mr. Sun said, "I am very strong, too. I can make flowers and plants grow. And if a little girl doesn't eat her ice cream cone quickly, I can melt it. Here is a chant about me." Then Mr. Sun said, "Mr. Sun, I'm the man. If I can't do it, nobody can."

Let's say Mr. Sun's chant together.

> Mr. Sun, I'm the man.
> If I can't do it, nobody can.

Mr. Rain said, "Let's have a contest to find out which one of us is the strongest."

Mr. Wind said, "Good idea. What shall we do?"

Mr. Sun said, "See that little girl down there with the pink jacket on? Every day she walks down this sidewalk to school. Let's see who can make her take off her jacket first. But we need a time limit for our contest. We will count to ten very slowly, and she has to take her jacket off by the time we're done."

Mr. Wind and Mr. Rain agreed. Mr. Rain said, "I'll go first. This will be easy. Watch this."

He said, "Mr. Rain, I'm the man. If I can't do it, nobody can. Friends, start counting."

Do you know what Mr. Rain did? Yes, he rained on the little girl. At first, he rained very softly, with small raindrops gently falling. **(Fold paper and cut from 1 to 2. Show oval piece as raindrop.)** But the little girl just kept on walking. So he rained harder. The little girl did not take off her jacket, instead she stopped to zip up her jacket and put up her hood.

All this time, Mr. Sun and Mr. Wind were counting the seconds up to ten. Can you count with them? They counted very slowly. "One… Two … Three … Four … Five … Six … Seven … Eight … Nine … Ten!"

Mr. Wind said, "Mr. Rain, you rained as soft and as hard as you could, but you did not get her to take off her jacket. Now it is my turn."

He said, "Mr. Wind, I'm the man. If I can't do it, nobody can. Now start counting, but count very slowly."

Mr. Sun and Mr. Rain started to count very slowly, "One… Two …" Mr. Wind started to blow very gently, but the little girl did not take off her coat. **(Cut from 3 to 4.)** So Mr. Wind blew harder. "Three … Four … Five …" Still she did not take off her coat, instead she wrapped her arms tightly around herself and bent her head into the wind. So he blew as hard as he could. "Six … Seven … Eight … Nine … Ten!" **(Cut from 4 to 5, and show half circle as wind.)**

Mr. Wind was all out of breath. He said, "I give up. I can't make her take off her coat. But then neither could Mr. Rain. Now it is your turn Mr. Sun. I bet you can't do it either."

Mr. Sun said, "Mr. Wind, I have never seen you blow so hard. You really did try, but you just could not do it. So, the best is last. That's me!"

He said, "Mr. Sun, I'm the Man. If I can't do it, nobody can. Count slowly to ten and watch how I do this."

Mr. Sun started to shine. **(Cut from 6 to 7.)** At first he just shone gently, but the little girl just kept on walking—she was almost to school by now. Mr. Rain and Mr. Wind started to count, "One … Two …" Mr. Sun shone a little brighter and a little warmer. "Three … Four … Five …" But the little girl kept on walking.

Finally, Mr. Sun shone a ray of sunlight down on the little girl with all of his brightness and all of his heat. **(Cut from 7 to 8 and display ray of sunlight.)** The little girl stopped walking. She put down her book bag. She unzipped her jacket and she sat down to rest. She wiped her forehead with her hand. Then she began to … Do you know what she did next? Yes, she took off her jacket!

Mr. Wind and Mr. Rain yelled the rest of the numbers as fast as they could. "Six … Seven … Eight … Nine … Ten!" But they were too late. The little girl had taken her jacket off and stuffed it in her book bag. She stood up, brushed herself off and walked quickly the rest of the way to school.

As she entered her classroom, the teacher said, "Marie, you are late! What took you so long?"

Marie answered in a surprised voice, "I'm late? Well, first it rained as I was walking, and then it was so windy that I had trouble even standing! Then the sun came out, and I got so hot that I had to sit down and rest. I had to take off my jacket. Why? How late am I?"

How many minutes did the teacher say that Marie was late? **(Unfold one and zero and show number 10.)** Yes, she was ten minutes late.

The teacher answered, "Marie, you are ten minutes late! But we don't mind. We all thought that it was going to be cloudy and rainy today and now the sun is out!" **(Hold yellow 10 against blue piece of paper.)**

All of the children said, "Mr. Sun, he's the man. If he can't do it, nobody can."

Mr. Wind and Mr. Rain smiled at the children's silly joke. But Mr. Sun just beamed with delight!

Activities

1. Compare and contrast several other versions of this tale about the contest between the sun and the wind.

2. Discuss how the other elements of weather might involve themselves in this contest. Let children share their ideas about snow, sleet, mist or fog getting involved in this contest.

3. Sing the song, "There Were Ten in the Bed and the Little One Said."

4. Practice counting from one to ten and back down from ten to one.

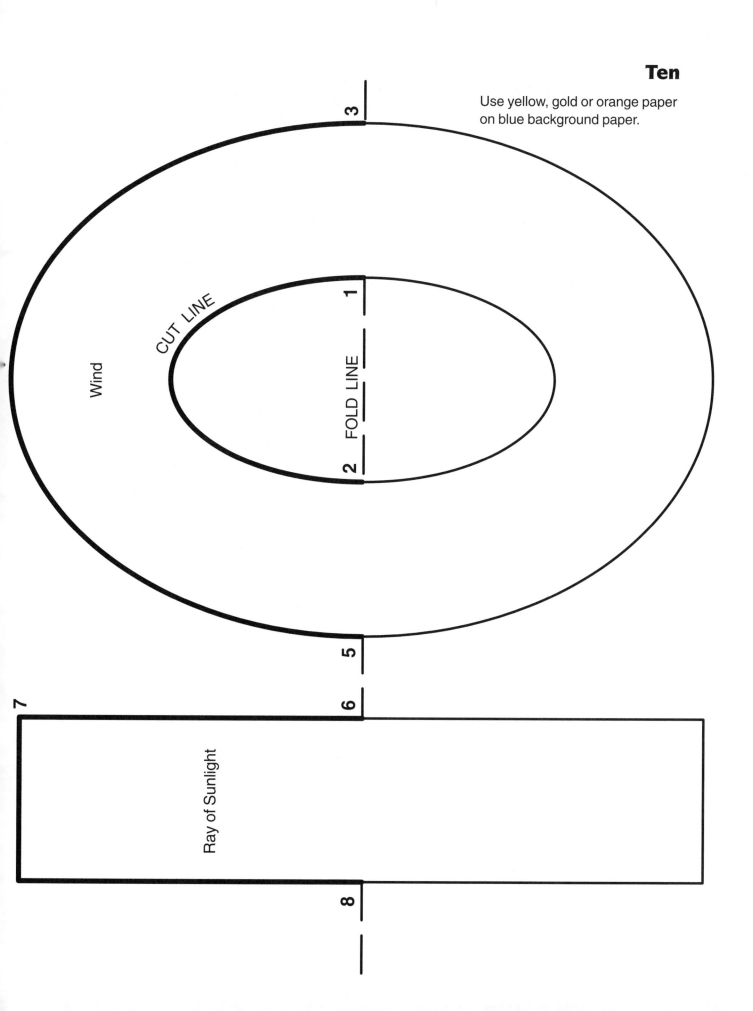

Ten

Use yellow, gold or orange paper on blue background paper.

3

1

CUT LINE

FOLD LINE

2

Wind

5

6

7

Ray of Sunlight

8

One Hundred

How many days have you been in school? Is it more or less than 100 days? Do you have a "One Hundred Day Celebration" on the day that you have been in school for 100 days? Celebrating 100 days of school is a fun reason to have a party and there are hundreds of different activities you can do for your "One Hundred Day" Party.

Here is a story about a student and what happened to him at his One Hundred Day Party. Jack was just about your age, too. All week, his class had been getting ready for their One Hundred Day Party. They had done all kinds of activities with the number 100. Listen and see if you have done some of these same activities.

Jack and his friends painted a mural of a centipede with 100 legs. They measured and marked off 100 feet down the hallway from their classroom door. They sent and received e-mail greetings from 100 other schools across the nation. The teacher even gave a 100 percent to everyone on their last math test—after they corrected any mistakes they had made on the test. The school librarian had made a huge book display of 100 of her favorite books. The janitor counted out 100 soda cans to be recycled. Everyone brought in their old phone books, counted them in groups of 100 and then put them in the recycling bin. **(Cut from 1 to 2 for recycling bin.)**

Finally, after an entire week of "One Hundred" activities, the official One Hundred Day had arrived. Jack's teacher said, "As you know, we will have been in school for one hundred days this Friday. I want everyone to bring in 100 of something and show it to the rest of the class. You can bring anything you wish, just as long as there are 100 of them. Use your imagination."

Sean said, "I'm going to bring in my bottle cap collection in a bag." **(Cut from 2 to 3 for bag.)**

Julie said, "I'm going to bring in a bowl with 100 of my prettiest shells."

"Teeth," said Kara, with a laugh. "I'm going to bring in 100 teeth." Everyone groaned. Kara's dad was a dentist. **(Cut from 3 to 4.)**

Tom was silly, too. He shouted, "Banana peels, I'm going to bring in 100 banana peels."

Jack did not say anything. He did not know what he should bring.

That night at supper, Jack's mom suggested lots of different things. She said, "Jack, there are lots of things you could take to school. You could take 100 rubber bands, 100 paper clips, 100 toothpicks. Do you like any of those ideas?"

"No, Mom. I want to take in something fun, something the kids would enjoy," said Jack.

Well, I can't think of anything else," said Jack's mom as she got up from the dinner table, walked over to the cupboard and pulled out her usual dessert. "I know you'll think of something."

Jack watched his mom stuff a handful of M&Ms into her mouth. He got an idea. Do you know what it was?

Yes, Jack decided to take 100 M&Ms to school. He got out a small sandwich bag and carefully counted out 100 chocolate candies. They smelled so good!

The next morning, Jack put the bag full of M&Ms in his pocket and started off to school. He was in such a hurry that he had forgotten to eat breakfast. He thought about those delicious M&Ms in his pocket. Do you know what he did?

Yes, Jack ate just a few. He thought that no one would notice if he had 98 or 97 M&Ms instead of exactly 100.

But can you eat just two or three M&Ms? No, and neither could Jack. He just kept eating two or three at a time and before long, guess what happened!? Yes, that's right. All 100 of Jack's M&Ms were gone. His pocket was empty. **(Cut from 5 to 6 to show empty pocket.)**

Now what was Jack going to contribute to the One Hundred Day Party? He had to think of something to do with one hundred. Everyone in the class was excited to show what they had brought for One Hundred Day. Finally it was Jack's turn to stand up and show his 100 of something. Slowly he stood up. He had a pair of scissors in his hand and a piece of paper. He started to cut the paper but the teacher interrupted him.

"Jack, where is your 100? Did you bring anything?" the teacher asked.

Jack answered, "Yes, I did. But I need to tell you a little story about my 100 thing. Actually, I did start out this morning with 100 items. But I got hungry. Can you guess what I brought to school?"

All of the time that Jack was talking, he was cutting his paper. **(Cut from 7 to 8.)** The other kids all tried to guess what he brought but they did not guess the correct thing.

Jack said, "You all had good guesses but not the correct one. I will just have to show you what I brought." Jack held up his folded paper. He showed everyone the letter that he had cut out. **(Show letter m.)** What letter did Jack cut out? Why?

Jack said, "This letter "m" stands for the 100 M&Ms that I ate on the way to school."

Jack's teacher said, "So Jack, now you don't have anything to contribute to our 100 collection, right?"

Jack said, "Oh, but I do have something to contribute. And here it is!" **(Unfold paper and show number 100!)**

Activities

1. Do some of the activities listed in the story.

2. On a large piece of paper, let everyone draw enough smiley faces to equal 100.

3. As a class, count out 100 items, take 100 steps, stand on one foot for 100 seconds, do 100 jumping jacks.

4. Draw a caterpillar with 100 body parts, or 100 legs, or both!

One Hundred

Use lilac, pink or purple paper.

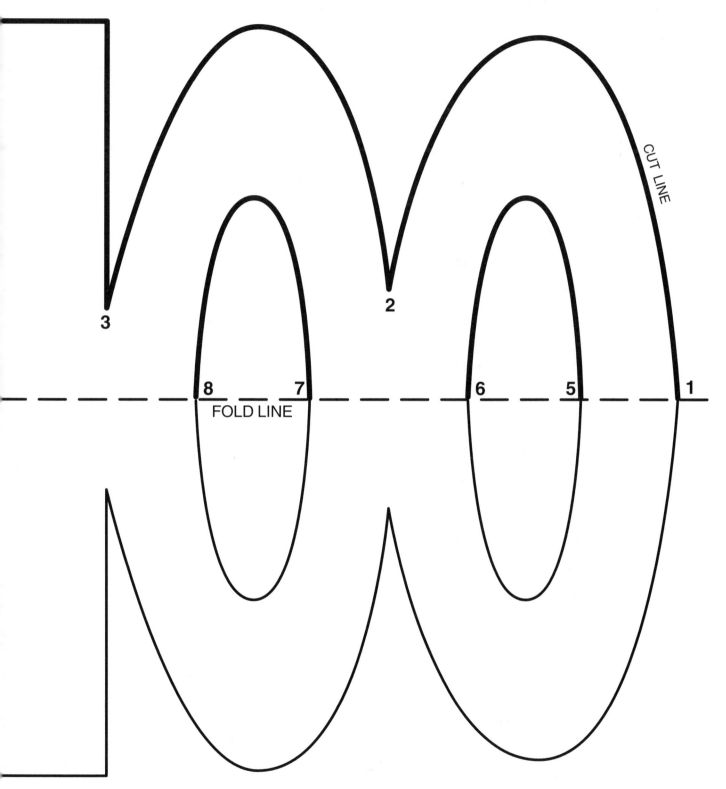

CUT LINE

3

2

8   7   6   5   1

FOLD LINE

Number Review

Raccoon loved to trick Bear. It was his favorite thing to do. And Bear was so easy to trick. One day as Bear was walking by, Raccoon started moaning and groaning, "Ohhhh, Owwww, oh no."

Bear stopped and said, "Why Raccoon, what is the matter? Are you hurt?"

Raccoon said, "One … Two … Three–Four–Five, once I caught a fish alive. Six … Seven … Eight–Nine–Ten, then I let him go again."

Bear said, "Why did you let him go?"

Raccoon said, "Because he bit my finger so."

Bear said, "Which finger did he bite?"

Raccoon said, "The little one on the right."

Bear said, "Wow. That's a nice little rhyme Raccoon. Let's say it again."

Can you say that nursery rhyme with me? I'll point to each number as we come to it. **(Repeat rhyme.)**

Raccoon said, "Bear, I really want to show you which fish it was that bit me."

Bear said, "All right."

Raccoon said, "But Bear, remember the rhyme—then I let him go again."

Bear asked, "Why did you let him go?"

Raccoon said, "Because he bit my finger so."

Bear said, "That's right. I remember now. Which finger did he bite? I forgot."

Raccoon yelled, "The little one on the right."

Bear said, "Oh, yeah. I remember now. Was it a pretty fish?"

Raccoon said, "Pretty? Pretty dangerous, if you ask me. Listen Bear, I really want to show you that fish."

Bear said, "But you just said that you let him go."

Raccoon answered, "Yeah, I did let him go. Hey, I've got an idea. Why don't we both put our fishing poles back in the water and try to catch him again?"

Bear said, "Oh, I don't really want to go fishing right now."

Raccoon said, "But Bear, I really want you to see that fish. You have to know what he looks like so that if you ever catch him, you will know that he will try to bite your finger."

Bear said, "Can't you just describe the fish to me?"

Raccoon said, "No, I have to show him to you. Come on, it won't take us long to catch him again."

So Bear and Raccoon sat down to fish. Bear caught the first fish. He pulled it out of the water and said, "Is this the fish that bit your finger?"

Raccoon pretended to look the fish over very carefully. Then he said, "No, that is not the fish."

Bear started to throw the fish back into the water.

Raccoon yelled, "What are you doing, Bear? Don't throw that fish back. Then you will have to catch it again. Here, I will help you by putting the fish in my bucket."

A short time later, Bear caught another fish. "Is this fish the one that bit you?"

Raccoon pretended to look it over very carefully. Finally he answered, "No, that is not the fish either. Just give him to me and I will put him in my bucket. I do not seem to be having any more luck fishing today. Bear, you just keep on catching those fish and putting them in my bucket. I think I will just take a little snooze right here."

Bear fished all afternoon and Raccoon slept all afternoon. Bear caught lots of fish but he did not want to wake up Raccoon and ask him to look at each one, so he just kept putting them in Raccoon's bucket.

By the end of the afternoon, Raccoon's bucket was full of fish, and Bear was tired and hungry.

Raccoon woke up and saw his bucket full of fish. He said, "Wow! Bear, you are a great fisherman. Did you catch the one that bit me? Let's see here. Well, you know, there are so many fish in this bucket that I am going to have to take it home and look over each fish carefully. I will let you know tomorrow if you caught the right one."

Bear said, "I could take some fish home with me and look for that particular fish. I am very hungry."

Raccoon said, "That is so nice of you to offer to help me but I don't want you to go to any trouble. Anyway, you don't know what the fish looks like, and I would not want him to bite you." Bear had to agree with that.

Raccoon picked up the bucket of fish and went home to make himself a big fish dinner, and Bear just went home hungry, never knowing that he had been tricked.

Let's say the poem together one last time. **(Point to numbers as you say them.)**

One … Two … Three–Four–Five, once I caught a fish alive.

Six … Seven … Eight–Nine–Ten, then I let him go again.

Why did you let him go?

Because he bit my finger so.

Which finger did he bite?

The little one on the right.

✨ Activities

1. Recite this nursery rhyme again reviewing and emphasizing all the numbers. Give each child a photocopy of the following number page and let them point to each number as they say the poem with you. They could use markers or crayons to trace each number.

2. Show several different books of nursery rhymes. Find this particular poem in the other books. Compare and contrast other things about the book—the artwork, number of poems, size of the book, etc.

3. Discuss the rhyming words in this poem. Are there other words that rhyme with bite, go, five, ten?

4. Encourage children to paint or draw a picture of their favorite part of the story. Discuss how Raccoon tricked Bear.